P9-AOT-942

DISCARD

Regional
Dictionary
CHICANO ^{of}
SLANG

Regional Dictionary of CHICANO SLANG

Dr. Librado Keno Vasquez
Maria Enriqueta Vasquez

Jenkins Publishing Company
The Pemberton Press
Austin 1975

REFERENCE

PC
4829
S6
V3

Copyright © 1975
Jenkins Book Publishing Company, Inc.

Library of Congress Catalog Card No. 75-3721

Dedication

We give our deepest thanks to our parents, Mr. and Mrs. Fernando Canche Sr. and Mr. and Mrs. Ventura Vasquez, who have given fully and unselfishly of their time for us during the completion of our Text.

To all of the Chicanos in the United States with whom we have shared our dreams and vented our frustration, those with whom we have invested our most basic feelings and whom we have loved most and hated most, we acknowledge their most important influence on our professional development and personal life.

In addition to our indebtedness to the above unmentioned contributors, we give our sincere thanks to those who have given fully and unselfishly their time for us, and regardless of our differences, their unrestrained personal and emotional commitment to our Chicano way of life. A deep sense of gratitude is due to our friends and colleagues, Dr. Arthur Pearl, Mr. Ruben Reyes, Dr. George I. Sanchez, Mr. Joe Farias, Dr. Robert Nardelli, Mr. Abelardo Betancourt, Dr. John Hansen, Ralph Groener, Dr. Clarence Schmicke, Mr.

Andres (Andy) Gomez, Dr. William E. Drake, Mr. Alfonso Alamia Jr., Dr. Douglas E. Foley, Mr. Gus Segade, Dr. John M. Rich, Alurista (Chicano poet), Dr. Thomas D. Horn, Mr. Gus Getner, Dr. David Ballesteros, Mr. Carlos Velez, Dr. Alberta Castaneda, Dr. Arthur Moelhman, Dr. John Laska, Dr. J. Stephens Hazlet, Professor Carlos I. Calderon, Dr. Arnulfo Martinez and Dr. Americo Paredes.

Finally, to our daughters and only son, Doria, Yliana, Michelle and Kenito, for their unhesitating personal humiliating sacrifice and understanding toward the completion of our Text.

L.K.V.
M.E.V.

"Yo grite por la dignidad
pero nadie me escucho."

Keta Vasquez

Author's Explanation

The First Regional Dictionary of Chicano-Hispano Americano Slang (dialects) spoken in the Southwest (Diccionario Regional De Dialectos Chicanos-Hispanos Americano Hablados En El Suroeste) is the result of an urgent demand on the part of the tri-ethnic communities to have a rather more concise and extensive list of genuine regional speech variants that might be considered "essential" in the education of our Spanish-speaking community. This manuscript was formerly initiated several years ago before reaching the form in which it is here presented. Numerous individuals have aided us greatly in the final choice of format for the list that you now have in your hands.

Our Dictionary has been designed to facilitate Educators, Civic-minded individuals, Farmers, Government, State officials, and other personnel with the essential communication skills in Oral-linguistic Chicano Spanish. In order to arrive at a more scientific selection of Chicano vocabulary words, many of these unrecorded extraordinary words are questionable for inclusion in any basic vocabulary list, and no professional teacher would be willing to accept them as the basis of departure of their Spanish instruction without having a "word count" extended to a more adequate (Textbook Spanish) number.

Emperically speaking, it is our contention that a vast amount of the monolingual and or tri-lingual population in the United States, particularly in the Southwest definitely do not know how to communicate orally with the majority of the unrepresented population of Chicanos, Puerto Ricans, Cubans, Central and South Americans. The art of Oral communication in different dialects (speech variants) and or idioms are indeed complex because of the differences of regional native dialects spoken by each specific group of Spanish-speaking people. We do not profess to be experts in the area of structured linguistics; however, we are cognizant of several regional native speech variants spoken in Southern Texas, California, and other populated areas with a tremendous concentration of Spanish-speaking people. We have often heard educators say that only those who have studied the area of linguistics and are well-informed of the theory format are the only individuals who know and should be writing about Regional dialects. We disagree with this theory; instead, those who have lived and spoken such idioms should be the legitimate authors. It should be noted that each specific regional area in the Southwest has laid claim to being the "first" to have initiated these unrecorded and or published speech variants (Chicanismo). Each regional theory is open for criticism and it is indeed debatable. We have spoken and witnessed some of the disputed Barriology terminology considered derogatory, in nature, for nearly thirty years; however, it should be noted that Professor Aurelio Deleon came out with a segment of words nearly forty years ago. Numerous others have followed, but not to the extent of a combination of Spanish and English. Regardless of which regional area actually should accept the "honor" or "credit" for such an ingenius contribution to our structured linguistically oriented society; a portion of the contribution should be attributed to our Mexican immigrants from the Republic of Mexico and the ingenius Linguistic work of Aurelio DeLeon, a Mexican Professor in Mexico.

We have compiled this brief Chicano-Hispano Americano Slang Dictionary for the purpose of providing an easy tool of Oral communication in Barriology terminology. It should also be clearly understood that an undetermined amount of Spanish-speaking people do not consider nor accept the Slang terminology as the proper "diction" to be utilized in the education of their children. Others will say that the above "specific" group do not represent the entire Chicano population. Whatever the case might be, it will attempt to bridge the educational gap of the Spanish-speaking population. The Slang Dictionary will provide our uninformed population with a variety of speech variants (Dialectology) in a non-sophisticated pattern to be utilized in their efforts to communicate and articulate effectively with our less-fortunate American citizens. The authors have no intentions of providing the "solution" to the linguistically different American in relationship to their education; instead to provide a brief-concise guide in the art of communication in specific essential idioms (dialects) that seem more appropriate. These dialects consist of our native "Tex-Mex," "Calo," "Pachuquismo," "Cali-Mex," and other speech variants that are constantly being created daily by the influx of Spanish-speaking people. The critical issue centers around dialectology. According to Webster, a dialect is "a variety of a language that is distinguished from other varieties of the same language by features of phonology, grammar, and vocabulary, and by its use by a group of speakers who are set off from other geographically or socially." We may have then geographical dialects such as Bostonian, East Texas and Alabamian, etc., or social dia-

lects such as the language of the "**Bato Tirilongo.**"
Perhaps of major importance is the student's point of
view, and it is emphasized that those selected list of
words are indeed a student's list, not a list primarily
designed to impress the Academy of languages. This
Slang Dictionary will include numerous non-standard
Spanish words, their English definition, regional
usage, and some brief examples of how to utilize
these terms monolingually and trilingually.

This Regional Dictionary contains hundreds of Bilingual words and phrases that have never been
printed in a dictionary form.

The Regional Chicano-Hispano Americano Slang
Dictionary is as simple as an elementary book that
does not need a structured index to thumb through;
nor is it time consuming when moving from page to
page before being able to find the proper diction of
each term. It will also contain an English word index
with a Spanish meaning. We are cognizant that
numerous linguistic investigators have made tremendous inroads in the area of dialects; however, more
research needs to be done and published in the area
of Chicano dialects. With this concept in mind, the
beachhead has been laid for Chicano Researchers to
continue the dialectology challenge. It is our hope
that the individuals utilizing this Chicano Slang Dictionary will read, learn, and criticize it with
discernment and receptivity.

*The Chicano Slang Dictionary definitions do not have
the full concensus approval of all the Spanish-speaking people in the United States. It should be understood that each geographical area has its own distinct connotation of Barriology Terminology.

Introduction

Historical Perspective of Dialectology. This "Regional Dictionary of Chicano-Hispano Americano Slang Spoken in the United States" will be concerned with the social, cultural, and educational dialectology and the effect its teaching has on the racial situation in this country. In this area of technology and social consciousness educators are realizing that our dominant society (culture) is neglecting the education of Spanish speaking children because they cannot be understood. Nearly several million Mexican Americans in the United States, particularly in the Southwest, have the statistical reputation for speaking substandard (slang) Spanish. What is the definition of substandard Spanish? The non-standard Spanish which most of us speak are regional dialects (e.g., Tex-Mex, Calo, Pachuquismo). Regional dialects are synonymous to drug addiction because these people depend on their daily idioms to communicate effectively with their immediate family and friends. For the benefit of the reader who feels confused with the term "Dialects," the authors will attempt to clarify the definition by utilizing Haugen's definition which specified that:

"All languages have dialects. The so-called 'standard' is but itself a dialect and in many language areas there are both regional standard dialects (e.g., London vs. Mexico City vs. Buenos Aires), and non-standard dialects in the same areas, each with its regional hue. Furthermore, language is constantly changing, indeed nowhere faster than among 'standard dialects'; and many of the features of present 'Non-Standard' dialects simply represent survivals of elements which were once in 'Standard' use rather than, as is so often erroneously assumed, corruptions of the standard."

The learning of a regional dialect makes an understanding of the nature of the language problem of the Spanish speaking people. However, this understanding of "Chicano" dialects does not exist at present. It is the primary objective of this concise dictionary to bring about this essential understanding which is lacking among our educators.

For additional clarification, the National Council of Teachers of English (N.C.T.E., Task Force Program, 1965, p. 9,272) makes it perfectly clear that, "The unfortunate and unavoidable fact is that some of the English dialects are so unique as to prevent speakers from participating fully in social structure, in propriety, in the distinct culture, or in the democracy of the United States. . . . Teachers everywhere recognize that social economic mobility require that a person be able to speak an "established" dialect, or standard, informal English." It is evident that millions of Spanish speaking people in the United States do not speak "Standard" Spanish (e.g., Textbook Spanish). They speak a mixture of "Totacha" which consist of English, substandard Spanish, and other regional dialects combined with a Spanish accent. These combination of words make up the different unique speech variants. Those regional dialects mentioned previously (Tex-Mex, Calo, Pachuquismo) are becoming the inspiration of the contemporary Spanish-speaking communities in the United States. Mexican Americans in the United States are constantly developing new "words," which are then transformed into their own regional usage. Theodore Anderson, among others, has pointed out how the school's failure to teach English as a Foreign Language and also to teach written Spanish has produced illiterates in both languages.

Before entering into the presentation of the "Regional Slang Dictionary," it is well to examine factors which contributes to the language impediment of Chicanos in the Southwest. Studies have uncovered the reason why the oral-drill method of teaching English grammar has failed. "The existence of these divergent grammatical forms (McDavid and Austin, N.C.T.E., 1965, p. 13,272) has long been recognized in the schools; the traditional treatment, however, has been in terms of lapse, errors, and deviations, with no recognition that they are part of a regular system." Chicano language (speech variants) is not, as we formerly thought, standard English with substandard deviations, but rather a complete system that allows its users to express themselves clearly to those with whom they speak. The teaching of English to Spanish-speaking students must therefore adopt a new method. We must utilize and teach these children the language (dialectology) they will need when they enter our educational systems.

Other studies indicate that the linguistic handicap is an important learning problem of the Non-English speaking student. Just what is the extent of this linguistic handicap which is so important in determining the school success of the Mexican Americans. Numerous studies and investigations report that, as of 1930, (El Paso, Texas) probably more than 90 percent of the Americans of Mexican origin entering school in Texas could not understand and speak

English (Manual, 1930, pp. 120-121). Similarly, in Denver, 31 percent of the Mexican parents spoke Spanish at home and 17 percent of the parents born in the United States utilize no English at home (Colorado Board of Education, 1937, p. 6). While Giddings found that pupils in Kindergarten, grades 1, 1b, and 2, in a predominantly Spanish speaking school in Los Angeles, California, compared favorably with English-speaking children (Giddings, English Elementary Review, Dec. 1929, pp. 269-272) of the same level in other respects, they suffer from a definite language handicap since few had heard any English at home. Educators and Idiomists in the field of language disabilities among the Spanish-speaking population, can be easily concluded that an analysis of the language problem as to the nature of the difficulty faced by Mexican American children is a basic one.

This concise dictionary will not attempt to pretend that it is an exhaustive analysis of the subject. Rather, it has been undertaken as a "beachhead" to further explore the mechanics of linguistics. It is a matter of common knowledge that Chicano children face serious difficulties in adjusting themselves to school work conducted in the English language. Spanish-speaking children are undoubtedly influenced by the fact that "Spanish (e.g., regional dialects) are their native language. That is to say that, since "Standard English" is the native language of the dominant culture (school), they are confronted by a trilingual tricultural situation (e.g., Standard English, Standard Spanish and Substandard Spanish). Dr. Mandler asserts that "One of the biggest drawbacks of standard I.Q. tests is that results depend on a child's vocabulary. Most minority children have a language problem. It's more obvious with Spanish-speaking (Mandler, San Diego Evening Tribune, June 16, 1970, p. X-18) kids, but applies to black kids as well. Their language vocabulary is different from the language on standardized tests. A test may ask the child to identify a toboggan by circling the appropriate picture; the test will show a toboggan; a sleigh, and a wagon. A child may not know what a toboggan is but that doesn't mean the child is not bright." It's well-documented that these educational problems extend throughout the United States. This means that all of us within our own regional districts (geographically) must assume the responsibility of promoting the area of Spanish dialectology (idioms) in the classrooms as a definite beachhead plan and solution of an immense problem.

This new dialectology method goes under the term of trilingualism and triculturalism. Its aim is first to equip the Spanish-speaking child with a systematic pattern of his own regional dialect while allowing him to operate at his own pace in his second and third language (e.g., Standard Spanish and English); and last to teach him. Such teaching should be informal at the beginning) in an effort to provide a substitute for the characteristic language learning process where children arriving from various communities pick up the local idiom (McDavid Austin, N.C.T.E., 1965, pp. 13,245) from older children in their neighborhoods. Teachers in this artificial situation must recognize a discrepancy between the "target pronunciation" in the schools and the home pronunciation and avoid stigmatizing the latter. The aim is "functional bi-dialectalism" with children able to switch codes as the occasion demands. Dr. Thomas D. Horn, Chairman of Curriculum and Instruction at the University of Texas and a strong proponent of bilingualism, is one of those educators who in recent years has begun to express doubt about the effectiveness of bilingual programs as implemented in many Texas school districts. "We need to chart an intellectual road map for each child, to tell us where the child is in relation to the destination of oral language proficiency (Horn, Austin American Statesman, Aug. 20, 1972, p. B-2). The child's language ability should be identified when he enters school and periodically his progress should be evaluated. Our current language instruction, where exists, has been largely a well-meaning effort, aimless and unprofessional, an exercise in frustration for children and futility for teachers." He also expressed deep concern with the qualification of the teachers handling numerous bilingual programs. This seems to many concerned educators to be the major problem in our educational system.

Before concluding the introductory section of this Chicano Slang Dictionary, it should be mentioned that Spanish-speaking children often receive a conflicting, weakened personal and national identity because they are getting a diluted dose of Spanish and English composed of the unqualified and traditional teachers. With the above in mind, this particular educational problem among the Spanish-speaking children should be bridged by the utilization of regional dialects (speech variants) as a means of classroom instruction. It is our contention that it will promote social and economic mobility without desecrating the Chicano racial and cultural pride. Teachers will have to respect the students' regional dialects as part of him, yet assist him to choose the appropriate language for his particular situations.

Probable Origin Stages
of Chicano
Regional Dialects
1000 A.D. - 1972 A.D.

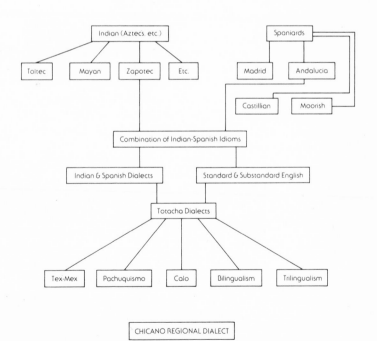

Indian (Aztecs. etc.)					Spaniards	
Toltec	Mayan	Zapotec	Etc.	Madrid	Andalucia

Castillian   Moorish

Combination of Indian-Spanish Idioms

Indian & Spanish Dialects   Standard & Substandard English

Totacha Dialects

Tex-Mex   Pachuquismo   Calo   Bilingualism   Trilingualism

CHICANO REGIONAL DIALECT

Accepted 1975

15

Pronunciation Guide

A	a	a		N	n	ene
B	b	be		Ñ	ñ	ene
C	c	ce		O	o	o
Ch	ch	che		P	p	pe
D	d	de		Q	q	cu
E	e	e		R	r	ere
F	f	efe			rr	erre
G	g	ge		S	s	ese
H	h	hach		T	t	te
I	i	i		U	u	u
J	j	jota		V	v	ve
K	k	ka		W	w	deble ve
L	l	ele		X	x	equis
Ll	ll	elle		Y	y	ye, i griega
M	m	eme		Z	z	zeta, zeda

Vowels
a, o, u, e, i (y)
ah, oh, oo, ay, ee

Vowel Combinations
ua, ue, ie, ei
wah, way, yay, ayee

Numbers 1-20

1. Uno	(oo-noh)	11. Once	(ohn-say)
2. Dos	(dohs)	12. Doce	(doh-say)
3. Tres	(trays)	13. Trece	(tray-say)
4. Cuatro	(kwah-tro)	14. Catorce	(kah-tor-say)
5. Cinco	(seen-ko)	15. Quince	(keen-say)
6. Seis	(sayees)	16. Diez y seis	
7. Siete	(syay-te)	17. Diez y siete	
8. Ocho	(oh-choh)	18. Diez y ocho	
9. Nueve	(nway-vay)	19. Diez y nueve	
10. Diez	(dyays)	20. Viente	(vayeen-tay)

Days of the week

Domingo	(doh-meen-goh)	Sunday	Lunes
Lunes	(loo-nays)	Monday	
Martes	(mahr-tays)	Tuesday	
Miercoles	(me-air-coless)	Wednesday	
Jueves	(hway-vays)	Thursday	
Viernes	(vyayr-nays)	Friday	
Sabado	(sah-bah-doh)	Saturday	

Months of the year

Enero	(ay-nay-roh)	January
Febrery	(fay-bray-oh)	February
Marzo	(mahr-soh)	March
Abril	(ah-breel)	April
Mayo	(mah-yoh)	May
Junio	(hoo-nyoh)	June
Julio	(hoo-lyoh)	July
Agosto	(ah-gos-toh)	August
Septiembre	(say-tyaym-bray)	September
Octubre	(oh-too-bray)	October
Noviembre	(noh-uyaym-bray)	November
Diciembre	(dee-syaym-bray)	December

Abbreviations

Abbreviations
N.: Noun
Derog: Derogatory
Slg: Slang
V: Verb
S.W.: South West
U.S.: United States
T.M.: Texas-Mexican
C.M.: Cal-Mex
Tot: Totacha
Def: Definition
Orig: Original
Pop: Popular
Bilig: Bilingual
Arz: Arizona
Tex: Texas
N.M.: New Mexico
Cal: California
U.O.: Unknown Origin
M: Mexico
N.S.: Non-Standard
L. A.: Latin American
Countries
S.T.: South Texas
M.T.: Mestizo (Indian-
Spanish)

A

ABANICO - An electric fan, etc. T.M., M., S.W.

ABARCADOR - Hair pin set. T.M., M., S.W.

ABENTON - A lift, a push and or/a ride. T.M.

ABOCANO - To run anxiously. T.M., M., S.W.

ABRE LA BRECHA - Get out of my way and/or make path. T.M., S.W.

ABUJA - A needle. T.M., S.W.

ABUJERO - An opening; a hole. T.M., S.W., M.

ABUSADO - Sharp, alert, and/or on the ball. T.M., S.W.

ACHICOPALADO - An individual who is hung-up on the contemporary youth movement of today. S.W.

AGACHADO - To bend down and/or lower one's part of the human body. T.M., S.W.

AGASAPADO - A person who hides and/or is in hiding for specific reasons in order not to be seen. T.M., S.W.

AGARRAR PATADA - To get a kick of, usually after someone plays a specific trick. T.M., S.W.

AGRINGADO - Anglocized, such as an Anglocized Mexican-American who normally speaks English and does not follow the tradition. T.M., S.W.

AGRITO - To yell and/or cry out loudly. T.M., S.W.

AGUADOR - Water Boy, an individual who follows the current in terms of politics. T.M., S.W.

AGUANTAR LA VARA - An individual who sticks to his convictions regardless of what might happen to him. T.M.

AGUAS - To be careful, to watch out, and/or waters. T.M., M., S.W.

AGUILA - Watch it and/or be careful. T.M., S.W.

AGUITADO - Very tired, frustrated, disgusted. T.M., S.W.

AGUITAR - To frustrate an individual by any means. T.M., S.W.

AGUITARSE - Low morale, tired and/or nervous. T.M., S.W.

AHORITA - Right now at this moment. T.M., S.W.

AHUICHOTIAR - To encourage a person. T.M., S.W.

AIDANELA - A personal name of a female meaning Nelly. T.M., S.T.

AIGRE - Pure air and/or fire up an individual. T.M., S.W.

AISCREAM - Ice cream. S.W., M.

AL ALBA - Alert, on the ball. T.M., S.W.

ALAMBRE ELECTRICO - A thin, skinny individual; an old saying pertaining to a person who seems malnutrition. T.M., S.T.

ALCAUETE - Encouraging someone to do something unusual. T.M., S.W.

ALELUYA - A name given to an individual who belongs to another church other than the Catholic (Church of Christ) (Assembly of God) (Pentecost, etc.) T.M., S.W.

AL FOMBRILLA - Measles (German). T.M., S.W.

ALGODONERAS - Freeloaders, won't steal to feed habit. S.W.

ALINEADO - He in the right with the law. T.M., S.W.

ALIVIANADO - An individual who is high on drugs. T.M., S.W.

ALIVIANAR - To assist, to lend a hand/and or to help out. T.M., S.W.

ALIVIARSE - Childbirth. T.M., S.W.

ALO - Hello, are you there. T.M., S.W.

AL OTRO LADO - Across the border on the Mexican side. S.T.

AL TROTE - To walk at a fast pace and/or to trod. T.M., S.W.

AMACHADO(A) - A stubborn individual who will not under any circumstances change his mind. T.M., S.W.

AMACHINAR - To strike, to get on with it. C.M., S.W.

AMANSAR - To tame an individual. T.M., S.M., S.W.

AMARADO - Tight down, married. T.M.

AMARIO - A city in West Texas, Amarillo, Texas. T.M., S.W.

AMARRADO - A person who is considered married and/or called for already. T.M., S.W.

AMERICANO - Normally considered an Anglo-Saxon; English-speaking surname. T.M., S.W.

AMOLADO - A sick person (sickness) and/or an individual who is financially broke. T.M., S.W.

ANCLIAR - To settle down in one particular place. T.M., S.W.

ANDA CHUECO - Doing illegal transactions. T.M., S.W.

ANDAR AHUITADO - Frustrated, feeling of frustration. T.M., S.W.

ANDARIEGO - An adventurer, traveler and/or a person who is not stable. T.M., S.W., M.

ANDAR LOCOTE - High on drugs. T.M., S.W., C.M.

ANDAR SOLARES - To be alone; to walk by thyself. T.M., C.M.

ANDAR VOLANDO BAJO - An individual who is under the influence of drugs and or considered to be feeling extremely blue. T.M., S.W.

ANDAS MUY PLOCHA - You're neatly dressed. T.M., S.W.

ANIMAS - Hope something happens; a wish. T.M., M., S.W.

ANONERA(O) - One who exaggerates extremely. T.M., S.W.

ANTIOJOS - To be observable in nature and/or bifocals, glasses. T.M., S.W.

AOLER - To smell for odor, etc. T.M., S.W.

APAGADORA - A fire engine. T.M., S.W.

APALANCARSE - To get a hold of something valuable. T.M., S.W.

APANAR - To steal, buy and/or get a hold of something. T.M., S.W.

APAPACHAR - To encourage an individual to pursue an objective regardless of whatever happens. T.M., S.W.

APATIN - A walk on foot; without an automobile. T.M., M., S.W.

APERLADO - Normally a Chicano with light skin (not brown nor white). T.M., M., S.W.

APLASTARSE - To sit down and not move at all. T.M., S.W.

APLOGAR - To simmer down, to calm down. T.M.

APLOMO - To wait around stubbornly. T.M., S.W.

APURON - An individual who loves to harrass people whether on the job or not. T.M., S.W.

ARAIZA - The State of Arizona. S.W.

ARANARSE - To get married. T.M., S.W.

ARISCO - A person who does not trust anyone and/or an individual who is excessively jealous. T.M., S.W.

ARRANAR - A very stubborn person. T.M.

ARREJUNTADOS - Living together as man and wife. T.M., S.W.

ARREMPUJONES - To move a person by pushing him. T.M., S.W.

ARRENDARSE - To come back after taking those initial steps forward. T.M., S.W.

ARREQUINTADO - A person who has drank enough and is walking extremely weird and/or an individual who pressures people. T.M., S.W.

ARRENQUINTAR - To corner an individual (e.g., a fight, argument). T.M., S.W.

ARREQUINTARSE - To be cornered, not being able to move around. T.M., S.W.

ARRIAR - To drive an automobile. T.M., S.W.

ARROLIAR - Let's go for a walk. T.M., S.W.

ARTURO PERLA - A former Professor at the University of Oregon who turned out Chicano Ph.D., in 1968-69. S.W.

ASERSE GARAS - Going out of your way and/or doing something constructive to achieve a task under any circumstances. T.M., S.W.

ASORILLAR - An individual with an injured/and or hurt ego. T.M., M.

ASQUELA - A mosquito. S.W.

ASUAVIZAR - To simmer down, take it easy. T.M., S.W.

ATACON - An individual who insults someone verbally. T.M., S.W.

ATARANTADO - Absent-minded, having difficulties with reality. T.M., S.W.

ATASCADO - Stupid, good for nothing and worthless. S.W.

ATENIDO - A person who depends on someone else for any given situation. T.M., S.W.

ATIRANTADO - An individual who is dead. T.M., S.W.

ATIZAR - To hurry and/or to turn the fire over and/or to move at a faster pace. T.M., S.W.

A TODO DAR - An expression used meaning it's O.K. and all right. S.W.

A TODO GUELO - An expression used for approval. T.M., M., S.W.

A TODO MADRE - An expression used for approval. S.W.

ATONTADO - An individual who does things without thinking about the consequences. T.M.

ATORNILLADO - A term meaning a person and/or individual packing common sense. S.W., T.M.

ATOTONDRA - A mixed-up female and/or irresponsible person. S.W.

ATRABANCADO - A careless person. T.M., S.W.

ATROCIDADA - A female who takes advantages of any situation. T.M., S.W.

ATROCIDADO - A male who takes advantages of any situation. T.M., S.W.

AUROPLANO - An airplane. T.M., S.W.

AVENTADO - An individual who is well-versed and fully-prepared in every capacity. T.M.

AVENTAR A LOCO - To ignore someone and/or someone in particular. T.M., S.W.

AVIENTALO A LEON - To ignore completely a person or individual. T.M., S.W.

AVISPA - A bee. T.M., S.W.

AVOLAR - Get out of here and/or scram. T.M.

AY TE GUACHO - See you later. S.W., S.T.

AZTLAN - Original homeland of the Nahuatl nation (Aztec tribe) in the Southwest. S.W., M.

AZODONIAR - To hoe the ground area. T.M., S.W.

AZOTO - He gave in; paid his debts to society and/or was forced into submission. T.M., S.W.

AZUL - A policeman and or/cop. C.M., S.W.

B

BABICHE - (derog.) S.O.B. Son of a bitch. T.M., S.W.

BABOSO - Imbecile, stupid and or/an idiot. T.M., S.W.

BACHA - A cigarette butt, small and/or short butt. T.M., S.W.

BAISA - An individual hands, working hands, heavy. T.M., S.W.

BAJAR - To lower one self into a specific level of one's life, a feeling of demotion within one self. T.M., S.W.

BALDE - A hobo . S.T.

BALE - A taxi driver. S.T.

BAQUIAR - To back-up another person. T.M., S.W.

BARBIAR - A person who is considered a Brown Noser, an individual who does things for other persóns. T.M., M.

BARBON - A heavy beard and/or an individual who is considered a tough person. T.M., M.

BARRIGA - Stomach, chubby and/or a beer belly. T.M., S.W., M.

BARRIO - A neighborhood, community area of Chicanos, at one time considered a derogatory term meaning Red Light District (Prostitute Area). S.T., T.M., S.W.

BARRON - A person who thinks in terms of wealth and material items. C.M., M.

BATATIRILI - A Pachuca, a woman zoot-suiter as referred by some Chicano. C.M., M.

BATE - A baseball bat. T.M., S.W.

BATO - A guy referred by the Chicanos. S.W., T.M.

bato loco - Among the Chicanos, he is considered a cool guy. S.W., T.M., C.M.

24

BATO TIRILONGO - A sharp Chicano and/or dude. S.W., C.M.

BASQUETBOL - American basketball. T.M., S.W.

BEBE LECHE - Hop Scotch, a typical Chicano pastime for children, such as for amusement purposes (game). T.M., S.W.

BEIS - A base (baseball). T.M., S.W.

BENDIDO - A Chicano (Mexican-American) considered a sell-out; turn coat, and a Chicano who tends to lean toward the Anglo's way of life. S.W.

BERRINCHUDO(A) - High tempered person. T.M., S.W.

BESOTIO - He kissed her all over. T.M., S.W.

BESTIA - An unhumane individual. S.W., M.

BETABELERO(A) - A sugar beet picker. T.M., S.W.

BETABELES - Sugar beets. T.M., S.W.

BICA - Money. T.M., S.W.

BIEN CERRADO - A narrow-minded person. T.M.

BIEN DADO - A healthy individual. T.M.

BIEN JARAMILLAS - A stubborn person. S.W.

BIL - A bill and or a dollar bill. T.M., S.W.

BILLETERA - A bill-fold, a place to keep cash. S.W., M.

BIRONGA - A word meaning beer in South Texas, alcoholic beverage. S.W., T.M., S.T.

BIRRIA - Alcoholic beverage meaning beer; in Mexico (Guadalajara) it is considered a dish (food) tender goat. T.M., M.

BIROTE - French bread specially made by Chicanos. T.M., M.

BISQUETE - A biscuit. T.M., S.W.

BLANQUILLO - An egg (food). T.M., S.W.

BLOAUTE - Blow-out tire. T.M., S.W.

BLOFE - A bluff. T.M., S.W.

BLOFIAR - To bluff someone. T.M., S.W.

BLOQUE - A cement block. T.M., S.W.

BOCON - Loud-mouth. T.M., S.W.

BOGUE - A horse buggy. T.M., S.W.

BOICOTIAR - To boycott. T.M., S.W.

BOISA - Hand. T.M., S.W., C.M.

BOITELAS - Hey, what's happening! T.M., S.W.

BOLA - A crowd and/or gathering (group of people). S.W.

BOLAS - A lot of things to do. T.M., S.W.

BOLERO - Shoe shine boy, a youngster who shines shoes. M., S.W.

BOLEVIAR - To dance. T.M., S.W.

BOLIAR - To shine shoes. T.M., S.W.

BOLILLO - A term meaning Anglo-Saxon white given by Chicanos. T.M.

BOLO - An individual who has left the scene of a specific area, to fly away and leave. T.M., S.W.

BOLSA - A purse and or a hand-bag. T.M., S.W.

BOLSUDA - An individual with money. S.W.

BOMBA - A balloon. S.W.

BOMBARDIAR - A derogatory term meaning going to the restroom and/or toilet to do number one or two. T.M.

BOMBAS - A military weapon (bomb). T.M., S.W.

BOMBO - A very tired person and/or tiresome individual who has just done some heavy physical work. S.W.

BOMBOS - Fireman and/or fire fighters. T.M., S.W., M.

BOMPER - A car bumper. T.M., S.W.

BONCHE - A group and or a bunch of people. T.M., S.W.

BORDO - A dike and/or flood water trap. T.M., S.W.

BORLO - A happy gathering such as a party and/or dance. T.M., S.W.

BORLOTIAR - An individual who loves to attend parties. T.M., S.W.

BORLOTERO - Instigator, one who agitates another person. S.T.

BORRACHALES - A person who drinks frequently. T.M., S.W.

BORRADOR - An eraser (Pencil Blackboard). T.M., S.W.

BORRARSE - To scram, move out. S.W., S.T.

BORRATE - Scram, get away, take off. T.M., S.W.

BOS - A bus. T.M., S.W.

BOSLAIN - A bus terminal. T.M., S.W.

BOTARSE - To move out and/or to leave. T.M., S.W.

BOTEA - A bottle. T.M., S.W.

BOTANA - Referred to as a beer appetizer, usually meat roll in a tortilla. T.M., M., S.W.

BOTAR - To kick and/or get rid of a person, to fire. T.M.

BOTI - A term meaning jail, normally used by those Chicanos in Arizona, California, and parts of New Mexico. S.W., C.M.

BOY - Frequently used as a nickname (Hecto, Arturo, etc.). S.W., T.M.

BRECAS - Automobile brakes. S.W.

BREQUIAR - To put-on the brakes. T.M., S.W.

BRODA - Brother. T.M., S.W.

BRONCO - A stubborn individual, tough and/or untame. T.M., S.W.

BRUJIAR - People who tend to go out at night. T.M., S.W.

BRUTAL - Extremely good. T.M., S.W.

BUENOTE - A good looking Chciano. T.M., M.

BUEY - Bullock, ox, and or stupid. T.M.

BUFA - A term meaning beer, such as when one in South Texas tells another Chicano, let's go to drink beer. T.M., S.W.

BUQUIAR - To book (gambling); horse betting. T.M., S.W.

BURRO - A term often referred to a slow learning person. T.M., S.W.

BURRON - An individual considered unintelligent. T.M., S.W.

BUSCAR PEDO.-To look for trouble, trouble maker in the sense of the term. T.M., S.W.

BUSCAS MOSCAS - A trouble maker and or a Dennis the menas. T.M., M., S.W.

BUSCATOQUE - A person who desires and/or wants and needs drugs. S.W., C.M.

BUSCON - An individual who desires a certain position at the expense of others. T.M., S.W.

BUSGA - Normally referred to as female dog and/or a female who overeats. T.M., S.W.

BUSGO - A person who eats tremendously, overeating. T.M., S.W.

BUSQUITA - A small female dog. T.M., S.W.

BUTLEGAR - A bootlegger. T.M., S.W.

C

CABALLO - A person considered clumsy. T.M.

CABRON - (derog.) Normally an individual whose wife is stepping out on him. S.W.

CABULIAR - To accomplish a designated task. T.M.

CABURRO - A cowboy and/or a Cowpuncher. T.M., S.W.

CABUS - A train, caboose. T.M., S.T.

CACA DE TORO - (derog.) Bull shit. S.W.

CACARA - A girl (crackler). S.W., C.M.

CACHAS - A noticeable facial expression indicating a sign of anger. T.M.

CACHETADA - A slap on the face and/or on the seat. T.M., S.T.

CACHETIAR - To slap somebody on the face. S.T., T.M.

CACHUCHA - A cap and/or a cover for the head. T.M., S.W.

CACHUDO - An individual in a bad mood (facial expression). T.M.

CACHUQUIAR - To double cuss. C.M., S.W.

CADI - A nickname for cadillac. T.M., S.W.

CAFE CON LLANTA - A cup of coffee with a doughnut. T.M., M.

CAFE CON MOSCA - A cup of coffee with some sweet Mexican bread.T.M.

CAFRO - A cup of coffee. T.M., S.T.

CAJETAS - Headache and/or an individual who is extremely disliked by other people. M., T.M., S.W.

CAJETUDA - A sexy female. T.M., S.W., M.

CAJONERO - An individual who makes fruit and/or vegetable cardboard boxes. T.M., S.T.

CALABACITAS - Little white lies. T.M., S.T.

CALABAZA - Stupid, pumpkin and/or the carburetor air cleaner. M., T.M.

CALABURNIA - Stupid and/or odd ball. T.M., S.W.

CALACA - Death, a sign of death. T.M., S.W., C.M.

CALATE - Try it, buddy! T.M., S.W.

CALAVERA - A stupid individual, not too bright. T.M.

CALCIAR - To walk without any shoes. T.M., C.M.

CALCOS - Shoes. S.T., S.W.

CALDIADO - An angry person with justification. T.M., S.W.

CALDIAR - Mad, uptight and/or fed-up. T.M., S.W.

CALDIARSE - To get real angry at an individual for specific and unknown reasons. T.M.

CALENTAR - Up-tightness, a heated facial expression. T.M.

CALENTURA - Referring to an animal and/or a human being, who are in heat (sexually), or high body temperature. T.M., M., S.W.

CALIFAS - California. Calif., C.M., S.W.

CALLEMOS GORDO - People are fed-up with us. T.M.

CALLO (ARCADIO) - Nickname for Arcadio. S.T.

CALMALA - To calm down and/or to have patience, wait awhile. T.M., S.W.

CALMANTES MONTES - A term meaning to take it easy, take life in stride. T.M., S.T., S.W.

CALMEROZ - Cool it, brother. S.W.

CALO - A Chicano idiom and/or speech variant normally used in California. C.M., S.W.

CALOTA - A good-looking female, a gal, really nice looking. T.M., S.W.

CALOTE - An individual who is considered strong in the area of politics. T.M., S.W.

CALVITO - God. S.W., C.M.

CALZONES - Male trousers and/or female panties. N.M., T.M., S.W.

CAMBALACHE - To exchange goods and or items. S.T., S.W.

CAMELLAR - To work. S.W., T.M.

CAMILLA - A bed and/or a pad. T.M., S.W.

CAMPIAR - To camp out and/or a cook-out. T.M., S.W.

CANALERO - A ditch rider (water canal). T.M., S.T.

CANDILAR - To lure an individual into a trap and/or to blind him with a bright light. T.M., S.T.

CANTON - House and or home. S.W., T.M.

CANUTO - Nickname for Kenneth Canche, a boy born in Dixon, New Mexico. N.M., T.M., S.W.

CAPA CAIDA - The closing of an individual's eyelids. T.M.

CAPACETE - The roof of an automobile. S.T., T.M.

CAPIAR - To get a hold of, to cooperate. T.M., S.W.

CAPIROTADA - A delicious dish (cheese, bread, raisins) made by most Chicanos in the Southwest. S.W., T.M.

CAPIRUCHO - Captain as referred by some Chicanos in the U.S. T.M., S.W., M.

CAPON - An individual who cannot conceive and/or bear children, due to some undetermined nature. T.M.

CAPOTIAR - To catch an undetermined item. T.M., S.W.

CARCACHA - An old automobile, such as a model-T car. T.M.

CACAJIAR - To laugh loudly. S.T., T.M.

CARANCHO - Tricky, sly fox and/or a person with a deviate behavior. T.M., S.W.

CARGAR LA CARRETA - Carry the load. S.T.

CARILLA - A person who does their job in a hurry and/or is forced to move at a faster pace. S.W.

CARINOSO - A kind-hearted person, likable. T.M., M., S.W.

CARITA - Flirt and/or a teaser (female). T.M., S.W.

CARNAL - A Chicano soul brother. T.M., S.W.

CARNALA - A Chicano soul sister. S.W.

CARNALONGO - A big brother. C.M., S.W.

CARRAZO - A real shiny and expensive car. S.T., S.W.

CARRETILLA - A wheelbarrow. S.W.

CARRO - An automobile car and/or a means of transportation. S.W.

CARRUCHA - An automobile and/or a car. T.M., S.W.

CARTERA - A means of personal identification, such as a passport. M., T.M., C.M.

CASCARIAR - To be using his last resources. T.M., M.

CASITAS - Rest rooms, odd-houses and/or toilet. T.M., S.W.

CATIADO - An individual who is physically and brutally attacked. T.M., S.W.

CARIARLO - To beat him up physically. T.M., S.W.

CATIZA - A person who has been beaten-up physically. T.M., S.W.

CATOS - A physical fight followed up by heavy blows. T.M., S.W.

CELEFAN - Cellophase paper. S.T., S.W.

CEROTE - A tall individual, normally over six foot. S.W.

CERVECERO - A person who drinks excessively. S.T., T.M.

CHAFA - A worn-out individual. C.M., S.W.

CHAFLAN - An early Mexican comedian from Mexico during the 1930's and 1940's. M., T.M.

CHAIN - Shine (on shoes). T.M., S.W.

CHALANES - Shoes. S.T.

CHALE - A term meaning "**No**" period. S.W., M., T.M.

CHAMBA - A job and/or an employment. T.M., M., S.W.

CHAMBERLINE - A male who escorts a female to a wedding and or other functions. T.M., S.W.

CHAMBIAR - To work on any specific job. T.M., M.

CHAMPIONATO - A championship. T.M., S.W.

CHANATE - Coffee, a Negro and/or a Black. S.W.

CHANCLAS - Shoes, normally not new. T.M.

CHANCLIANDO - Dancing. T.M.

CHANCLIAR - To dance up a storm. T.M.

CHANCLON - A great dancer in the Barrio. T.M.

CHANGA - Referring to a female who is considered a tom-boy. Also, a funny female, comical in nature. T.M., M., S.W.

CHANGO - Monkey and/or to be alert. T.M., S.W.

CHANTARSE - To get married. T.M., S.W.

CHANTE - House, home, or pad. T.M., S.W.

CHANZA - An opportunity, mumps, parotitis. T.M., S.W.

CHAPARRA - A stocky, short female. T.M., M.

CHAPARRO - Shorty, a short or small individual. T.M., S.W.

CHAPAS - Chops. T.M., S.W.

CHAPETA - A diaper and also an earring. N.M., T.M.

CHAPETE - (derog.) A male's personal possession (female), physically, emotionally or otherwise. S.T., S.W., M.

CHAPO - Nickname for shorty. T.M., S.W.

CHAPUCERO - An individual who cheats (e.g., sports, school, etc.). S.W., T.M.

CHAPUSIAR - To defraud and/or to utilize trickery methods in any game to win. T.M., S.W.

CHAQUER - A bridal shower. T.M., S.W.

CHAQUETERO - A two-faced individual usually not trustworthy. T.M.

CHAQUETIARLO - To betray someone and/or a friend. T.M.

CHARA - A charter. T.M., S.W.

CHARCO - A small ditch with some water and/or a small creek. T.M.

CHARLARLES - To speak up to a group of people. T.M.

CHAVALA - A gal and/or a woman, commonly used in California and South Texas. T.M., S.W.

CHAVALO - A young Chicano from the Barrio. T.M., S.W.

CHAVALON - A child or a kid. T.M., C.M., S.W.

CHAVETA - A Mexican-American considered white in the inside and brown on the outside. M., SW.

CHAVO(A) - Boy friend and/or a girl friend and a young child and/or a kid. T.M., S.W.

CHENTE - A nickname for Vicent and/or Vicente; often means a person who doesn't have any sense. T.M.

CHEQUIAR - To check. T.M., S.W.

CHERIFE - A county sheriff. T.M., S.W.

CHICAGO - Restroom, toilet and/or a bathroom. T.M., S.W.

CHICANO - One of the oldest human beings in North America. Mestizos-Spanish-Indian mixture and/or other members of La Raza. S.W., T.M., M.

CHICAS PATAS - A term normally used by Chicanos meaning a Chicano, Mexican-American, etc. T.M., S.T.

CHICHE - Female breast. T.M., S.W.

CHICLE - A person who tags along without being invited. S.T.

CHICLOSO - An individual who tends to tag along without being invited. T.M., S.W.

CHICOTUDO - An extremely important character. T.M., S.W.

CHIFLADO - A ladies man. T.M., S.W.

CHIFLETAS - Indirect remarks about one's feelings. T.M., S.W.

CHIFON - Chiffon. T.M., S.W.

CHILIQUIPIN - The hottest pepper wildly grown by Chicano families (**chile pepin**) in their gardens. T.M., S.W., M.

CHILLAR - A loud cry and/or an outburst of an infant in terms of loud noises. T.M., M.

CHILLON - A cry baby and/or a loud person in nature. T.M., M.

CHINCHIRIN - A fruit named Tangerine. T.M., M., S.W.

CHINGOS - A whole lot. T.M.

CHIPIAR - Attempting to break the drug habit or to control it by breaking up the pattern of absorbing dope. T.M., S.W.

CHIPIL - A spoiled brat. N.M.

CHIPON - A spoiled infant and/or youngster inspired by his parents. T.M., M.

CHIQUERO - A hog pen and/or a dirty area. T.M., S.W.

CHIQUIARSE - Playing hard-to-get. T.M., S.W.

CHIRIO(N) - Dripping of any liquid such as ice cream, etc. T.M, S.W.

CHIROTIAR - An act of play by a youngster, climbing trees, etc. T.M., S.W., M.

CHISCOPATE (no te rajes) - Don't chicken out; do not back out. Calif., C.M.

CHISME - Malicious gossip, commonly considered normal and/or a way of life. S.W.

CHISMOLERO - A male tattletale. S.T.

CHISMOLIAR - To squeal and/or to tell on someone about their particular activities. T.M., S.W.

CHISPA - Pistol, lighter and/or a spark plug and/or a person is prepared for any given situation (lively female). T.M., S.W.

CHISQUIADO - A deviate individual. T.M., M., S.W.

CHITIAR - To cheat on a test, etc. T.M., S.W.

CHIVA - Afraid, chicken, and/or a term 'an individual who acts and looks afraid.' T.M., M.

CHIVAS - The personal belongings of an individual, clothes, etc. T.M., M.

CHIVATA - An old person within the Barrio. T.M., S.W.

CHIVATO - An individual whose peers consider him a chicken and/or afraid. T.M.

CHO - A show and/or a movie (theatre). T.M, S.W.

CHOCALA - A friendly handshake to assure another person of no ill-feeling toward him. T.M., S.W.

CHOCANTE - A hateful individual who does not appreciate his friends. S.W.

CHOCLE - A chalk. T.M., S.W.

CHOFERIAR - To drive a car. T.M., S.W.

CHONGUIAR - To get a hold of another person's hair, such as in a physical fist fight between females. T.M., S.W.

CHOPIANDO - Shopping. S.W.

CHOQUE - An automobile wreck. T.M., S.W.

CHORE - A small and/or a shorty individual. T.M., S.W.

CHOTA - A policeman, cop andor an officer of the law. M., S.W.

CHOTIADO - An indivdual who has been black-listed, marked by someone. T.M., S.W.

CHOTIAR - When one makes a fool of someone. T.M

CHOTIS - An individual who does or says the wrong thing when trying to explain something. T.M., S.W.

CHUCHA - A real mean individual. T.M.

CHUCHIAR - A tattletale. S.T.

CHUEY - A Pachuco term meaning Jesus. T.M., M.

CHULIAR - To caress and/or to say something delightful about his appearance. T.M., S.W.

CHULO - Handsome and/or in many instances a homosexual according to the Barrio. Also, a dog. T.M., S.W., C.M.

CHUPA CHARCOS - Snickers, canvas shoes. T.M., S.W.

CHUPAR - To smoke. T.M., S.T., S.W.

CHUTIAR - To shoot and/or to fire a weapon. T.M., S.W.

CIEN - A delicate part of the body; upper left and right side of the skull. T.M., S.W.

CIROL - A Chicano term meaning "**Yes.**" T.M.

CISCO (Francisco) - Nickname for Frank. T.M., S.W.

CISNERA - A female character who is a habitual liar. T.M., S.W.

CLAPIAR - To clap (using both hands); and/or to applause. S.T.

CLAVAR - To steal, and/or to nail down. M., T.M.

CLAVENTIN - To rob. S.T., T.M.

CLEMO - Penny. T.M.

COACHE - An athletic coach. T.M., M., S.W.

COCHOTA - Too fat. T.M., S.W.

COCO - The human skull, the head. T.M., S.W.

COCOLES - One of the Chicanos favorite dish (beans). T.M.

COCTEIL - A cocktail (a drink). S.T., S.W., M.

COLA - Probation. C.M., S.W.

COLERIAR - To borrow. C.M., S.W.

COLGAR LOS TENNIS - When a person hangs-up his profession and/or job or quits. T.M., S.W.

COLGAR LOS GUANTES - To give up physically, emotionally, and personally. T.M., S.W.

COLIAR - To pursue and/or grab a person by the seat. S.W., T.M.

COLOPIAR - To swing around the town during the night. S.W., C.M., S.T.

COLORADO - A red color (not rojo). T.M., S.W.

COLORIAR - To color with crayons, water paint, etc. T.M., S.W.

COLOTE - Refers to a female buttock. T.M., S.W.

COLUMPIO - A character who normally walks with weird swing or a person who wears overalls. T.M., M.,

COMADRONA - A non-trained midwife. M., T.M., S.W.

COMO TE IDO - How are you, complementary remark to a person. N.M.

COMPA - A very close friend, just like a brother. T.M., M.

CON COLA - Leaving prison with some parole status. Going somewhere with family (e.g., bringing kids along). C.M., S.W.

CON EL GORDO - Hitchhiking and/or to thumb a ride. T.M., S.W.

CONGAL - An area (hang-out) for prostitutes. M., T.M.

CON QUEBRADA - A person desiring an opportunity will only succeed if a certain break is afforded. T.M.

CONTROLAR - To control. T.M., S.W.

CONVERTIBLE - A pick-up truck. N.M.

COPIAR - To copy any material by cheating on an examination. T.M., S.W.

CORA - A girl friend and/or a person who is very dear to one. T.M., C.M.

CORCHOLATA - A bottle cap. T.M., S.W.

CORONA - A big shot in the Barrio. T.M., M.

CORRECTANDO - To correct an exam and/or a term paper. T.M., S.W.

CORRENTIA - Took off quickly ahead of time. T.M., S.W.

CORTADO - An expression used by some Chicanos meaning to put down another Chicano verbally. C.M., S.W.

CORTARSE - To alienate oneself from a group. T.M., S.W.

CORTO - A term meaning that an individual has done something extremely unusual. T.M.

COTORRIAR - To rap and/or to talk with a group of people. T.M., M., S.W.

COTORRO - A talkative person. T.M., S.W.

COSCORRON - To hit him on the head. T.M., S.W.

COYOTE - A person considered a half-breed Spanish Anglo, and/or often considered the youngest son of a family. N.M., T.M., S.W.

CRANQUE - To crank up an automobile. T.M., S.W.

CREPA - A toilet and/or a bathroom. T.M., S.W.

CRISMAS - An American holiday, Christmas. T.M., S.W.

CRISTAL - A Chicano city named Crystal City, Texas. S.T., S.W.

CRUZADO - A half-breed, half Anglo and Mexican. T.M., S.W.

CUADRO - A frame or picture; in an agriculture status, it means a field. S.W.

CUATA - Brother, friend and/or a twin sister. T.M., S.W.

CUATE - Friend, companion and/or buddy. T.M., S.W.

CUATES - Real good friends, buddies. S.W., M.

CUATRO BAROS - Four dollars and/or four pesos. T.M., S.W.

CUERDA - Big boss, a leader within a group, also a daring individual. T.M., S.T., S.W.

CUERNOS - A devilish individual, bad in nature. T.M.

CUERNUDO - An individual with buck teeth and/or with a long, skinny face. T.M.

CUEROS - The guys. T.M., S.W.

CUERPO - A woman and/or a gal. S.W., T.M.

CUETAZO - A gun shot. T.M., S.W.

CUETE - Pistol, gun and/or to be drunk. T.M., S.W.

CULERO - An odd ball, an individual considered indifferent. T.M.

CUQUIAR - To bake and/or to cook. S.T., S.W.

CURA - A fix, normally used among heroin users in the Barrios. S.W.

CURALES LOS CALLOS - To get rid of a hangover. S.W.

CURAR - To take a fix (drugs). T.M., S.W.

CURARSE - To make fun of a person without justification. T.M.

CURARSE DE EL - To make fun of an individual with intentions to humiliate a specific person. T.M., M., S.W.

CURCIO - G.I. Shits (derog.). T.M., M.

CURSI - A sour and/or lousy type of person or thing. C.M.

CUYA - A woman who has a reputation for having an ex-amount of children. T.M., S.W.

D

DAIME - An American dime, money. T.M., M.

DALE GAS - When an individual is working at a slow pace one often tells him to get with it, fast. T.M., S.W.

DANDO CARRILLA - Harrassing; harrassment. T.M., S.W.

DAR AIRE - To fire and/or get rid of by means of rejection. T.M.

DAR BOLA - To provoke an additional problem. T.M., S.W.

DAR CALABAZAS - To make a fool out of another person. T.M., S.W.

DAR LIJA - Referring to a job that needs to be perfected and/or polished. T.M., U.S., M.

DAR LUZ - The go-ahead sign and/or to proceed. T.M.

DAR MADERA - Psychofanting an individual by any specific means to obtain whatever is desired. T.M., S.W.

DAR SU CHEQUE - To dismiss, discharge, to say goodbye, and/or take leave. T.M.

DATILE - A date. T.M., S.W.

DE AGUA - When an individual or person receives something (item) extremely easy, such as an inheritance. T.M., S.W., M.

DE AQUELLA - Very good, extremely good. S.W.

DEDO - Give him the sign of the finger. (derog.) T.M., S.W.

DEITIAR - To date and/or to escort. T.M., S.W.

DEJILO - Going straight ahead and forward. T.M., S.W.

DELEN - Go ahead, straight forward. T.M., S.W.

DEPRIMIDO - A person who has exhausted his means, physically and/or mentally. T.M., M., S.W.

DESATINAR - To make an individual lose track or count of time, etc. T.M., S.W.

DESBORRADOR - A pencil and/or a chalkboard eraser. T.M., S.W.

DESBOMBADO - Somebody that's financially broke. T.M.

DESCHARCHAR - To discharge a person (military employment). T.M., S.W.

DESCOLGAR - To leave without notice. S.W.

DESCONTADO - An individual who is in exile and/or had to leave a place without choice. T.M., S.W.

DESCONTAR - To leave and/or move out, take off. T.M.

DESCONTARSE - To leave an area and/or move out of a specific area for specific reasons. T.M., S.W.

DESCUENTALO - Get rid of him, and/or push him out. T.M., S.W.

DESCUENTATE - Get the hell out of here, like quick. T.M., S.W.

DESDADO - A person and/or an individual who have lost a place in a society. T.M., S.W.

DESFLECHADO - A disoriented individual. S.W., T.M.

DESFROZAR - To defrost a refrigerator. T.M., S.W.

DESGARRIATE - Destruction of personal property. T.M., S.W.

DESGRANARTE - To tear apart. T.M., S.W.

DESMADRALOS (derog.) - A term by Chicanos indicating a usual remark for a victory and/or defeat. T.M.

DESMADRE (derog.) - A messed-up affair involving numerous situations. S.W.

DESPULMONARSE - To work himself out of a good health status (worn-out). T.M., S.W.

DESTETAR - Stop breast feeding a baby. N.M., S.T.

DESTONTIAR - An individual who has lost sight of direction. T.M.

DESTRAMPADO - A normal individual who has the tendency to do things without thinking about the consequences. S.W., T.M.

DETUR - To detour. T.M., S.W.

DIEGO - Ten cents in American money. T.M., S.W.

DIFUSORA - Radio station. T.M., S.W.

DIPA - A dipper (water). T.M., S.W.

DIPO - A depot (railroad, bus, etc.). T.M., S.W.

DISPARAR - To pay a bill for other people who are indeed financially embarrassed. T.M., S.W.

DISQIAR - To disk any portion of a land acreage. T.M., S.W., M.

DOMPE - A dump truck. T.M., S.W.

DOMPIAR - To do away with anything in particular. T.M., S.W.

DORIA - Dory, a girl from South Texas. S.T., S.W.

DRENAJE - A sewer and/or drainage. T.M., S.W.

E

EIT! - HEY! T.M., S.W.

EJELE - A term which means making fun of a person by visual harrassment. T.M., S.W.

EL AZUL - The policeman, a cop. T.M., S.W.

EL AZUFRE - A type of drug (usually heroin). S.W.

ELBA (El Barbero) - The barber. T.M., S.W., M.

EL BOTE - A jail and/or the can, the hole. T.M., S.W.

EL CANTON DE LA PERRA GALGA - Greyhound bus station. T.M., M.

EL CATRIN - A well-dressed male. M., S.W.

EL CHAMORRO - The calf (human body). M., S.W.

EL CHOCHE - Any Christian affiliated church. T.M., M.

EL CHOPINSEN - A term utilized by Puerto Rican meaning shopping center. P.R., U.S.

ELECTRICO - Being drunk. T.M., S.W.

EL ESCOBON - Guitar, a musical string instrument. S.W., C.M.

EL ES NARIZ - A noisy individual who normally inquires about the latest news. T.M., S.W.

EL FONO-The telephone. T.M., S.W.

EL GUARACHASO - A typical Chicano dance in the Barrio. T.M.

EL GUATO - One pack of marijuana. S.W.

EL HACE LA PERRA - He plays hooky and/or lazy. T.M., S.W.

EL JURADO - The law, policeman and/or cop. T.M., S.W.

ELOTE - There is no way. S.W.

EL OTRO CACHETE - Term referring to Mexico; the other side of the border. T.M.

EL MANIADO - A person who is limited in some capacity. S.W., C.M.

EL MONO - Movies, flick and/or theater. T.M., S.W.

EL PERRO - A mean and/or cruel person. T.M., S.W.

EL PESCUESO - The neck. T.M., S.W.

EL POSO - Restriction or isolation in a prison hole. S.W.

EL PROBRE - Juvenile Probation Officer. C.M., S.T., S.W.

EL RANCHITO - Correction institution for boys. S.W.

EL RIELE - A train. M., S.T., S.W.

EL TELEVI - Television. S.W., T.M.

EL ZAPATASO - A northern Mexican-Chicano type of dance. T.M.

EMBACHICHAR - To steal in a professional manner. S.W., C.M.

EMBARCAR - To take off and/or leave for an unknown destination. T.M.

EMBRUJADO - A bewitched individual due to some supernatural factor. T.M., S.M., S.W.

EMPACHO - A Chicano type of constipation. T.M., M., S.W.

EMPEDARSE - To get drunk. T.M.

ENANO - Midget and/or a small operator. T.M., S.W.

ENBUSCAS - In search of. T.M., S.W.

ENCAJAR - To blame an individual, an offense. S.W., S.T.

ENCANDIDARLO - To lure him and/or her. T.M.

ENCANICADO - Completely in love. T.M., S.W.

ENCANTONIADO - He's married and/or been married. T.M.

ENCHILADO - Real angry. T.M.

ENCUETARSE - To get drunk or stoned. T.M.

ENJETADO - Extremely moody (set facial expression). T.M.

EN LA TORRE - A person who was beaten physically, emotionally and/or intellectually. T.M., M., S.W.

ENLISTARSE - To enlist such as in the military service. T.M., S.W.

ENPELOTADO (derog.) - A male really in love. S.T., S.W.

ENTACUCHADO - A well-dressed Chicano in the Barrio. T.M.

ENTACUCHARSE - To dress up. T.M., S.W.

ENTRADO - Referring to a person who has been drinking beyond the normal stages. T.M.

ENTRALE! - Go ahead! T.M., S.W.

ERES UN PARCHE - An individual considered a leech or one who depends on someone for something. T.M.

ERJOSTES - Airline hostess. T.M, S.W.

ESA - Hey there! T.M., S.W.

ESCALOFRIO - Chills, colds, etc. T.M., S.W.

ESCANTE - A little while. T.M., S.W.

ESCAMAR - To be scared and/or to be afraid of. T.M.

ESCOR - A score in a game. T.M., S.W.

ESCRACHO - He scratched in a game. T.M., S.W.

ESCURER - Motor scooter. T.M., S.W.

ESCUSADO - Bathroom, toilet. T.M., S.W.

ESE! - Hey you! T.M., S.W.

ESELE - Hey you, hello there. T.M., S.W.

ESE ES MI GALLO - That's my hero. T.M., M.

ESPATIAR - To spot someone. T.M., S.W.

ESPELIAR - To spell (WORDS). T.M., S.W.

ESPINECHE - Spinach. N.M., T.M., S.W.

ESPRIN - Spring (season). T.M., S.W., N.M.

ES PURO COCO - A Chicano who is actually white in the the inside and brown on the outside. S.W.

ES PURO GUARACHE - A Chicano referring to a Mexican from across the border. T.M., S.W.

ESQUINCLE - An infant or young child. S.W., M.

ESQUINIAR - To back-up an individual regardless of the circumstances. T.M., S.W., M.

ESTA bIEN MARZO - An individual born in the month of March are often referred to as being crazy. T.M., C.M.

ESTACAR - To stack books, paper, etc. T.M., S.W.

ESTA CRUDO(A) - A hangover. M., S.W.

ESTA DE AQUELLA ENTONCE - Everything is all right, then. T.M., S.W.

ESTA DE AQUELLO TODO - Everything is out of sight. T.M., S.W.

ESTA DE MALAS - He's in a bad mood and/or had had bad luck. T.M.

ESTA JODIDO - He's messed up (mentally and/or physically). T.M.

ESTAMPA - Stamp (mail). T.M., S.W.

ESTANTABLAS - There are even and/or equal. T.M.

ESTA PADRE - It's cool! T.M.

ESTA PAPA - Whatever the case might be, it seems good. T.M., S.W.

ESTA PELON - It's extremely difficult. T.M., S.W.

ESTA PISTOLAS - He's extremely drunk. T.M., S.W.

ESTARER - A car starter. T.M., S.W.

ESTARIAR - To start an automobile. T.M., S.W.

ESTECHEN WAGEN - Station Wagon. T.M., S.W.

ESTIRA IGUAL - Cooperate, cooperation at the same level. S.T.

ESTIRO LA PATA - An individual has just died. C.M., M.

ESTOY QUE ME LLEVA EL DIABLO - I'm about to blow my top. S.W.

ESTRAMOS - Pants. S.W., C.M.

ESTROPOJO - A sponge and/or wash cloth. T.M., S.W.

ESTUFAS - You had it, brother. T.M., S.W.

ESTUFIANDO - Sniffing on the contents which might bring temporary relief from the need of a fix. S.W.

ESTULITO - A sitting stool. T.M., S.W.

ES UN ALZADO - An individual who keeps to himself, does not take any chances, very careful. T.M., S.W.

ES UNA MASA - a person considered a slow poke, fatty, etc. T.M., S.W.

ES UN TAQUACHE - A good for nothing individual and/or a not worthwhile person. S.T., S.W.

F

FACETA - Having a stuck up personality. T.M.

FACHAS - A sloppy-looking individual (dress code). S.T., S.W.

FACHOSO - Sloppy looking. C.M.

FAJA - Belt. S.W.

FANDANGO - A festivity and/or party. T.M., S.W.

FANIAR - To fan out (baseball). T.M., S.W.

FANTOCHA - Prima donna. T.M.

FARUCAS - Falfurrias, Texas, a small community in South Texas. T.M.

FARUCASVILLE - Falfurrias, Texas. S.T., T.M.

FEDERICA - Federal (police, troops). T.M., S.W.

FEDERICO(LOCO) - A lunatic whom people might consider out of his head. T.M., S.W.

FEILIAR - To fail an examination test. T.M., S.W.

FEMELI - The family. S.T., T.M.

FERIA - Money, coins in terms of cash. S.W.

FERIAR - Exchange of money and/or to give a person specific change. T.M., S.W.

FICA - Money and/or cash. T.M.

FICHIAR - Looking for money, loan, etc. T.M., S.W.

FIFI - An individual that apparently looks and acts feminine. S.W.

FIFIRUCHO - A feminine male character, behaves like a woman. T.M.

FIL - Baseball and football field. T.M., S.T.

FILA - Knife and/or switchblade. S.W., T.M.

FILDIAR - A baseball player who is playing the position of a fielder. T.M., S.W.

FILERA - Switchblade and/or knife. T.M.

FILORIAR - To knife and/or cut someone. T.M.

FINCAS - An orchard with fruits. M., T.M.

FISGIAR - To stare at someone intensively. T.M., S.W.

FISGON - A character who often stares at people. S.T., S.W.

FLATE - A flat tire. S.W.

FLATIAR - Flat tire. T.M., S.W.

FLET - A flat tire. T.M., S.W.

FLOCHIAR - To flush a toilet and/or a bathroom. T.M., S.W.

FLOJERA - Laziness, low activity. T.M., S.W.

FLOJIAR - To loaf around. T.M., S.W.

FLONQUIAR - To flunk a course, etc. T.M, S.W.

FLORINDO - A person considered a gay and/or a queer. T.M, S.W.

FLORTIAR - To flirt and/or to make a pass through an expression. T.M.

FLUATA - Skinny person. S.W.

LE FALLO - Fail and/or did not accomplish given task. T.M.

FOCOS - (Eye) glasses. S.W.

FORCITO - A little Ford (automobile). T.M., S.W.

FORTIGO - Automobile named Ford. T.M., S.W.

FRAJO - Cigarette. T.M., S.W.

FRAJO DE CEDA - Doped cigarette. S.W.

FREGADERA - Idiotic statement. T.M.

FREGADITO - A sly individual and/or a person who is financially embarrassed. T.M., S.T., S.W.

FREGAR - An individual who wants to take advantage of any given situation, such as a job, money, etc. S.T., S.W.

FRENOS - Automobile brakes. S.W.

FRENTAZO - A person who physically strikes another individual with his forehead. S.T., T.M., S.W.

FRESCO - A queer and/or a homosexual. U.S., S.W.

FRISCANDOLA - To search for a specific item or to frisk a female. T.M., S.W.

FRISES - Freezers. T.M., S.T., S.W.

FUCHEFUCHE - A person considered scared of something. S.T., S.W.

FUCHI - He's afraid. T.M.

FULIAR - To fool someone, make fun of him. S.T., S.W.

FUTBOL - The game of football. L.S., M.

FUTBOLERO - A football player. T.M., S.T., S.W.

G

GABARDINO(A) - An Anglo-Saxon from the U.S.A. T.M., S.W.

GABACHO - A derogatory term meaning Anglo-Saxon White. T.M., S.W., M.

GACHO - Don't be so crude. T.M.

GAITA - A trick and/or a trap. S.T., S.W.

GAJO - A little piece of something. S.T., S.W.

GALGO - Someone who is sickly looking. T.M.

GALLINA - Chicken. S.W.

GALLO - Macho; and/or unafraid; lucky shot; blood. T.M., S.W., C.M.

GALLON - A brave individual (machismo). S.T., S.W.

GANCHAR - To hook and/or to get a hold of something. S.T., S.W.

GANGA - Gang or group of peers. T.M., S.W.

GARAJE - A car garage. S.T., S.W.

GARAPATAS - Ticks (insects). S.T., S.W.

GARRA - Clothing. T.M.

GARRAS - Rags, old clothing. T.M., S.W.

GARRERO - Raggedy-looking individual and/or a messed-up place (crummy looking). S.T., S.W.

GARROTIAR - Pitcher's ball is being hit successfully and/or to strike at a specific object. S.T., S.W.

GARSOLE - A French word meaning a piece of cloth (hat style) to keep the sun away from the face. S.T., M., S.W.

GASOFA - Gasoline. T.M., S.W.

GASOFA BUENA - Premium gasoline. T.M., S.W.

GATA - Maid, and/or housekeeper. T.M.

GENTE DE COLOR - Negroes, colored people, etc. S.T., S.W.

GLUFA - Glue (e.g., to smell and/or to paste). S.W., C.M., T.M.

GOL - Goal; a score in a game. L.A., M.

GOLFO - Golf. T.M., S.W.

GOLIAR - A goal in basketball or football. S.T., S.W.

GOLPES - A flurry of punches by fist and/or a sporadic physical hard blows. T.M., S.W., M.

GOLPIZA - A physical beating. S.T., S.W.

GOMA - Gum. C.M., S.W.

GORUDO - An individual wearing a huge hat. T.M.

GOTIADOR - Eye, nose, and ear wash dropper. S.T., S.W.

GRADO - Grade. T.M., S.W.

GRANIZO - Hail (hail storm). S.T., S.W.

GRENA - Human hair, normally that of a Bato loco and/or a hippy. T.M., S.W.

GRIFA - Marijuana, grass. T.M, S.W.

GRINGA - Female Anglo-Saxon White. T.M., S.W.

GRINGO - Anglo-Saxon and/or white male person. T.M., S.W.

GROCERIAS - Groceries (food). T.M., S.W.

GUACHA - Look at it. T.M., S.W.

GUACHAME - Watch me. T.M., S.W.

GUACHATE - Watch out. T.M., S.W.

GUACHIMAN - A day or night watchman. M., S.W.

GUAFLERA - (guafol) - Waffle (pancakes). T.M., S.W.

GUAIN - Wine. T.M., S.W.

GUAINO - An individual who drinks wine excessively. T.M., S.W.

GUAIPER - Windshield wiper. T.M., S.W.

GUAMASO - Hard blow. T.M.

GUANTADA - A fist punch. T.M., S.W.

GUARDAFONGO - An automobile fender. T.M., S.W.

GUAY - This term is usually referred to as a person that gets in somebody's way. S.T., S.W.

GUAYIN - Wagon. T.M., S.W.

GUERCA - A young girl. T.M.

GUERCO - A young boy. T.M.

GUERINCHE - An individual with light complexion. T.M., S.W.

GUERO - An Anglo-Saxon (white). S.T., S.W.

GUEROS - Anglo-Saxons and/or whites. T.M.

GUERRA - War. S.W.

GUILA - (Califa) Skinny girl (tex-Mex) prostitute. T.M.

GUINCHIL - Automobile windshield T.M., S.W.

GUSJIAR - To eat and/or eating. T.M., S.W.

H

HAMBORGESA - An American hamburger. M., SW., T.M.

HAZME LA PARADA - Stand by me. T.M., S.W.

HIELERA - Refrigerator (Ice Box). T.M., S.W.

HIELERIA - An Ice Plant and/or a place where ice is processed (made). T.M., S.W.

HIELERO - An Ice Man (vendor). T.M., S.W.

HIERBAJAL - A field of weeds or brush. T.M., S.W.

HOCICO - Refers to a human mouth. T.M., S.W., M.

HOCICON - Big mouth. T.M., S.W., S.T.

HOMBLIGON - A heavy set person such as a fat or big belly individual. T.M., M., S.W.

HOMBRAZO - A tall, healthy individual. T.M., S.W.

HONDA - **The new trend of today. T.M., S.W.**

HORQUILLA - Clothes pin and/or often referred to as a pitching fork. T.M., S.W.

HOTELERO - A hotel owner. T.M., S.W.

HUATO - A person who loves and/or likes to participate in numerous activities. T.M.

HUELDIAR - To weld. T.M., S.W.

HUERCA - A young girl. T.M., M., S.W.

HUERCO - A young boy. T.M., M., S.W.

HUEVON - Lazy and/or an individual who does not work at all. T.M., S.W.

HUEVONIAR - To loaf around the job. T.M., S.W.

HUEVOS - An individual who has guts and/or intestinal fortitude. (derog.) T.M., S.T., M.

HUEZO - A ring, in an act of matrimony; indicating that a specific person is wearing a wedding band. S.T., S.W.

HUEZOS - A gambling game, dice. S.W., T.M.

HUILA - Prostitute, whore (e.g., loose female). T.M., S.W.

HUIRLOCHA - An old automobile. S.W.

HUIZA - Girl and/or gal. T.M., S.W.

HULES - Rubber shoes. T.M., S.W.

HUMADERA - Referring to an automobile who is letting out a lot of smoke and/or a smokey area (such as in a pool hall). T.M., S.W.

HUNGARO - A gypsy. T.M., S.W.

I

IDATOPAN - A character from the interior of Mexico during the early Bracero movement. M., S.T., S.W.

ILO - Gosh! T.M., S.W.

IMPONER - To spoil and/or be dependent upon. T.M., S.W.

IMPRUVIAR - To improve. T.M., S.W.

INCONTAX - Income Tax. T.M., S.W.

INDIADA - Referred to a group of people belonging to the same clan. T.M., S.W.

INTONADO - A person who keeps up with the latest news. S.W., T.M.

IRNOS - To go and/or to leave. T.M., S.W.

J

JACALERA - A female visiting her neighbors. T.M., S.W.

JACALERO - An individual who is a frequent visitor to neighboring homes. T.M., S.W.

JACALIAR - To visit one's neighbors. T.M., S.W.

JAIBOL - An alcoholic beverage, a highball. L.A., M., S.W.

JAIC - To hike and/or to walk. T.M., S.W.

JAIGUEY - Highway and/or a road. T.M., S.W.

JAINIAR - To go steady with a girl. C.M., S.W.

JAINO - A boy. S.W., C.M.

JALANDO - To be working. T.M., S.W.

JALAR - To work. T.M., S.W.

JALON - To pull back something. T.M., S.W.

JAMBAR - To steal. T.M., S.W.

JAMBORGUER - Hamburger. T.M., S.W.

JAMON TORTILLA - A straight forward person. T.M., S.W.

JANDO - Money, whether it's cash and/or in coins. T.M., S.W.

JARUCHA - A lively female, alert and hard working. (In Mexico it means a person from Veracruz. (S.W., M.

JASPIA - Hunger. S.W., M.

JATANA - Guitar. C.M., S.W.

JAULA - A jail and/or a detention center. C.M., T.M., S.W.

JEFA - A term meaning one's mother. S.W., M.

JEFE - A term meaning one's father. S.W., M.

JEFITA - A polite term when referring to one's mother. S.W., M.

JEFITO - A polite term when referring to one's father. S.W., M.

JEROL - A blow. T.M., S.W.

JETIAR - An individual in a bad mood. S.T., S.W.

JETON - Big butt and/or lips. T.M., S.W.

JIJO - A surprise expression. T.M., S.W.

JINCAR - To deliver a physical blow. T.M., S.W.

JODER - A term used by Chicanos meaning to take advantage of a particular situation. T.M., S.W.

JODIDO - A person in bad shape (physically or otherwise). T.M., S.W., M.

JOM - Home base (baseball). T.M., S.W.

JOMRON - Home run (baseball). T.M., S.W.

JONKY - Another name for Anglo-Saxon. T.M., S.W.

JONRON - A home run. S.W., T.M., M.

JUAGUA - A bus. Florida, N.Y., P.R.

JUARILEZ - Juarez, Mexico. S.W., T.M.

JUE - To go. T.M., S.W., M., N.M.

JURA - A cop and/or policeman. S.W., T.M.

JURADO - Policeman and/or cop. S.W.

JURANDO - To swear. T.M., S.W.

JURGUNIAR - To shake an individual. T.M., S.W.

K

KELA - Angie and/or Angelita. T.M.

KENEDE - Kennedy, Texas. S.T., T.M.

KENO - Eugene and/or Eugenio. T.M.

KETA - Henrietta and/or Enriqueta. T.M., M., S.W.

KINESVILLE - Kingsville, Texas. S.W.

KINO - Jake and/or Joaquin. T.M., S.W.

L

LABERINTO - A loud group of people trying to discuss the same subject at the same time. T.M., S.W.

LA BAICA - The bicycle. T.M., S.W.

LA BOLA - Group of people. T.M., S.W.

LA CABRA QUE DA LECHE - A person with a tremendous future and considered worthwhile. M., T.M.

LA CAPA - A capsule of heroin. S.W.

LA CARGA - A load or batch of heroin. S.W., T.M.

LA CONECCION - Having important connections. S.W.

LA COREA - Border Patrol. T.M., M.

LA COSA OTRA - Terp, medicine used as substitute for drugs. S.W., S.T.

LA CREPA - Rest rooms, bath room. C.M., T.M.

LA CURA - To take a fix or cure themselves temporarily from the need of the drug. S.W.

LA ESPIRINA - A perk-up elderly individual. S.T., T.M.

LAGRIMIAR - To cry on someone's shoulder. T.M., S.W.

LA HONDA - The contemporary life style. S.W., S.T.

LA JULIA - The ambulance. C.M., S.W.

LA JURA - The police and/or cop. T.M., S.W.

LA LEY DE LA CALLE - The law of the street and/or the Barrio. S.T., S.W.

LA LINIA - The telephone. T.M., S.T., S.W.

LA LLORONA - A siren, fire engine, patrol car. T.M., S.W.

LA MACETA, LA MANO (Tex) - Flower case. T.M., S.W.

LA MADRE - A girl, in some cases considered a prostitute. S.W., S.T.

LA MARCA - A Chicano who is blackballed by his own community and/or peers. S.W., S.T.

LA MATONA - The cruel and/or evil woman. M., S.W.

LAMBIACHE - A brown noser and/or a person who tends to do favors for others in return for something. T.M., S.W.

LAMBUZQUIAR - An individual who tends to eat after meals. T.M., S.W.

LA MIGRA - U.S. Immigration Service; border patrol. T.M., M., S.W.

LA MORA - Correctional institution for boys. S.W.

LA MOTA - The pot. S.W.

LA MOVIDA - A mistress other than a legal wife. T.M.

LA MOVIDA CHUECA - Illicit relationship (sex). T.M., S.W., M.

LAMPARIAR - To look. T.M., S.W.

LANA - Money, no set amount of coins and/or cash. T.M., S.W.

LANGARA - A crooked person and/or an individual considered sly. T.M., S.W.

LANUDO - An individual who has wealth. T.M., S.W.

LA PALOMIA - Closely-knitted group of people, crowd, gang and/or a group of friends. T.M., S.W.

LA PANZA - Stomach. T.M., S.W.

LA PATADA - Dear John letter a la Chicano style. T.M., S.W.

LA PLANA - An individual who possesses a fist of iron. S.W.

LA PLEBE - The gang – A group of individuals who are together. (New Mexico) S.W., M.

LA PONCHERA - Punch bowl. T.M., S.W.

LARGO - Sly; sneaky. T.M., S.W., M.

LAS NAGLAS - Buttocks. T.M., S.W.

LA SOPA - Being in prison; or serving a prison term. S.W., T.M.

LAS PARTES - Genitals. T.M., S.W.

LAS TROMPADAS - An exchanged fist fight. T.M., S.W.

LA TIMBA - Also one capsule of heroin. S.W.

LA TORSIO - He passed away. T.M., S.W., M.

LA TUNA - Prison at El Paso, Texas. T.M.

LA TURICA - When addict listens to others in potential places to find the connections. S.W.

LE APAGARON LOS FOCOS - An individual with a black-eye. T.M., S.W.

LECHE - A slick and or sophisticated individual. T.M., S.W.

LECHUDO - A heavy and/or strong dude. T.M., S.W.

LE ECHO MOSCA - To tease him or her. T.M.

LE ESTA PONIENDO - Having an illicit affair, physical and/or otherwise (putting the make) sex. T.M.

LE FALTAN TUERCAS - He is not all there (i.e., lunatic). T.M., S.W.

LENGONIAR - To talk, converse, and/or speak. T.M., S.W., S.T.

LENTODOS - Bifocals, eye glasses, etc. S.T., S.W.

LEP - To run a lap around the track field. T.M., S.W.

LE PATINA EL COCO - Crazy in the head. T.M., M., S.W.

LEPE - An individual whose features represent a short-legged and heavy-set person. S.T., S.W.

LE PUSO EL DEDO - To accuse and/or blame an individual, also to blacklist a person. T.M., S.W.

LES CALLEMOS GORDO - We bore them. T.M.

LE SUMBA - Sharp, a person who knows his subject matter well. T.M.

LEVANTE - An easy pick-up. T.M., S.W.

LEVANTO ACEITE - To blow-up steam (e.g., anger). T.M., S.W., M.

LEVANTON - To boost one's morale. T.M.

LEY DEL BARRIO - Law of the Barrio. S.W., T.M., M.

LIACHO - A bundle of something (clothers). T.M., S.W.

LIBRE - A taxi cab (e.g., free man just out of prison). T.W., T.M.

LICORIAR - To observe and/or to look. T.M., S.W.

LIDER - A leader. S.T., S.W.

LIMA - To degrade an individual slowly. S.M., S.W.

LIMBURGO - Edinburg, Texas. S.T., T.M.

LINEA - To tell a lie or myth. T.M., S.W.

LIPETICQUE - Lipstick. S.T., S.W.

LIQUIAR - A leak. T.M., S.W.

LIRA - A musical instrument normally called a guitar. T.M., S.W.

LIZA - A man's and/or boy's shirt. T.M., S.W.

LLANTA - Middle part of the outside of the stomach around the waist. T.M., S.W., M.

LLANTAS - A famous Gringo dish meaning doughnuts. S.W., C.M.

LLAQUE - Bumper jack and/or a car lift. T.M., S.W.

LOBICA - A city in West Texas named Lubbock, Texas. T.M.

LO CHARASQUIARON - An individual who was physically cut up; a person with a facial scar. T.M., S.W.

LO EN TABICARON - They booked him in jail (e.g., any specific charge). T.M., S.W.

LOGRONA(O) - To take advantage of a situation. T.M., M., S.W.

LONCHAR - To go eat lunch. T.M., S.W.

LONCHE - A term meaning "lunch." T.M., Ariz., Calif., S.W.

LONCHERA - Lunch box. T.M., S.W.

LONCHERIA - Lunch counter, sandwich shop or a taco stand. M., S.W., S.T.

LONDRE - Laundry. T.M., S.W.

LO NOQUIO - He knocked him out cold. T.M., M.

LO PELUQUIARON - He lost out in a gambling game. T.M.

LORENZO DE LEON - Larry Lyons. C.M., S.W.

LOS - A term meaning Los Angeles. C.M., S.W.

LOTE - One city lot (e.g., 50 x 160). S.T., S.W.

LUMBRE - Hard on things (e.g., wears things out easily). T.M., S.W.

LUMBRIS - A term referring to skinny people. T.M.

LUQUIS - A person considered out of their head, S.W.

LURIAS - Crazy boy and/or girl. C.M.

M

MACALEN - McAllen, Texas. S.T., S.W.

MACANIAR - To strike a person with a billy club. T.M., S.W.

MACETA - Refers to a human hand. S.T., S.W.

MACHO - An all-round man; a virile individual (male). S.W.

MACHIGUAR - To drive and/or to manipulate other individuals. T.M., S.W.

MACIZO - Bank. M., T.M.

MACUACHE - A person who is considered not worthy (in life). T.M., S.W.

MADERA - To sycophant, to boost up someone's morale. T.M.

MADERIAR - Psychofant, to build up a person's ego in order to secure a reward. T.M., S.W.

MAGACIN - A magazine. T.M., S.W.

MALETA - (derog.) - Human waste and/or luggage. T.M., S.W.

MAJADERO - A loud-mouth individual. M., S.W.

MALANCON - An individual who feels sick; possibly due to physical and/or an emotional disorder. Calif.-Mex., U.O., T.M.

MALAVERIGUADO - An individual considered disobedient in all respects. T.M., S.W.

MALA YERBA - Poor quality and/or not trustworthy. T.M., S.W., M.

MAL DE ARCO - Tetanus, lockjaw. T.M., S.W.

MAL DE OJO - Evil eye, a common and/or strong belief of some Chicanos. M., S.W.

MALDICIENTO - A person who cusses a lot. T.M., S.W.

MAL HIJO - A son considered a radical, not following Mexican traditional life styles. T.M.

MALIA - Sick or craving badly for a fix. S.W.

MALILLA - He left in a hurry. T.M.

MALO - A bad dude and/or person. S.W.

MALPASADO - An individual who does not eat regularly (meals). T.M., S.W.

MAMADOR - A person who receives some type of benefits without justification. T.M., S.W.

MAMAIS - To be receiving something without earning it. T.M.

MANCHA NEGRA - Black sheep of the family or uncasted. T.M., S.W.

MANEA - Brakes of an automobile. T.M., S.W.

MANIJAR - To drive a car. T.M., S.W.

MANOSIAR (derog.) - To manhandle such as gal and/or woman. T.M., S.W.

MANTILLAS - Baby diapers (cloth or disposal type). T.M., S.W.

MAQUINA - A car. N.M., M., S.W.

MARCA - A person who has a scar on his face. S.T., C.M., S.W.

MARCHO - Committed to a penal institution or having been convicted of an offense. T.M., M.

MARICON - A gay and/or feminish type of male. T.M, S.W.

MARIJUANA - Pot, grass, etc. S.W., S.T., T.M.

MARMAJA - A term meaning money and/or cash. T.M.

MAROMIAR - To lay out a trap and/or to dispose of an individual by means of trickery. T.M., S.W.

MARQUETA - Meat market. S.T., S.W.

MASA - A flabby individual, soft, loose. T.M.

MASOTA - Nice-looking female. T.M., S.W., M.

MATATENA - A children game often played with rocks and a rubber ball. T.M., S.W.

MAYATE - Afro-American, Black. T.M., S.W.

MECA - A gal and/or a woman in a bad mood. T.M., S.W.

ME CAI - I like him or her, very likable. T.M., S.T.

ME CAI ATRABESADO - Do not like a person and/or cannot stand him. T.M.

ME CAI MUY SURA - Something you can't stand. A person you can't stand. T.M.

MECANSO GANZO - An expression meaning "ready to accept the challenge." T.M., M., S.W.

MECHAR - To match (game). T.M., S.W.

MECHAS - Matches, such as to light a candle and/or fire. S.W., S.T., M.

MECHUDO - Hippy, long hair individual. S.W.

ME CUADRA - She he appeals to me. T.M.

MEJICLE - Republic of Mexico. S.W., C.M., T.M.

ME LLEVO EL TREN - I'll be damned. T.M., S.W.

MENTOLATO - Mentholatum. T.M., S.W.

MENUDO - Tripes, small and large intestines. T.M., S.W.

MERO BEBE - Number one in a given situation and/or the only one. T.M.

MESQUITES - Months, time spent in jail and/or correction institution. S.W.

METELE! ● Keep hitting him! T.M., S.W.

METICHE - Meddling. T.M., S.W.

MEXICAS - Aztec Indian tribe considered a Nomadic tribe. M., U.O.

MICAELA (Kela) - A girl named Michelle. S.T., S.W.

MIERDA - Referring to a person who is not worth-while, dirty. S.T.

MIGUEL - Means (d) or (me). T.M, S.W.

MILO (Emilio) - Nickname for Emilio. S.T.T., S.W.

MI PRIETA - Sweetheart, my love. T.M., M.

MIRAMONTE - To stare, look and observe. S.T., S.W.

MISION - Mission, Texas. S.T., S.W.

MISTIAR - To miss (such as hitting a ball). S.T., T.S.W.

MITOTE - A party and/or a celebration. T.M., S.W.

MOCHO - A Mexican soldier. T.M., S.W.

MOCOSO - A young man who has not reached the stage of supporting himself. T.M.

MOFLE - A muffler (e.g., car). T.M., S.W.

MOGOTE - Brush land (e.g., mesquite trees, cactus). T.M., S.W.

MOJADO - A Wet Back (Mexican season worker). T.M., S.W.

MOLAR - To bother an individual by a mild and hidden harrassment. T.M, S.W.

MOLLERA CAIDA - Fallen fontanelle. M., T.M., S.W.

MONA - Nickname for Ramona. M., T.M., S.W.

MONO - Tarzan, movies theatre. N.M., M.

MONDONGO (Menudo) - A Chicano favorite dish (food) after consuming a large quantity of alco-holic beverages. M., T.M., S.W.

MONTONEROS - To gang-up on one person and physically assault him. T.M., M., S.W.

MOQUIENTO - Sniffling or having cold-like effects in-between taking a fix. S.W.

MORA - An individual with a reddish face. T.M., S.W., M.

MORMADO - Individual with a cold (e.g., running nose, sore throat). T.M., S.W.

MORRA(O) - A short, chubby woman and/or man. C.M.

MOSCA - A type of harrassment, such as making fun of a person. S.T., S.W.

MOTA - Another term utilized for marijuana. S.W., S.T., C.M.

MOTIADO - Stoned by drugs and/or under the influence of drugs. T.M., S.W.

MOVER EL GUSANO - Craving which starts again first within the mind and then with the body. M , T.M.

MOVERLE - To move an issue faster. T.M.

MULA - A stubborn woman in the sense of the word. T.M.

MUSICA CHICANA - (A) Mexican theme (music); normally considered soul music (e.g., polkas, corrido, etc.) (B) A type of Mexican music originating in and during the Mexican Revolution of 1910. T.M., S.W.

MUY PANCHA - A person who dresses sloppy. T.M.

N

NACHO - Naturally and/or by all means, yes. T.M.

NAGUAS - Skirts; female dress. T.M., S.W.

NAILON - Nylon stocking and/or nylon. S.T., S.W.

NALGIAR - To spank someone on his seat. T.M., S.W.

NARANJAS - Term meaning "no." T.M., M.

NARANJILES - Nothing at all. T.M., S.W.

NEIL POLICH - Nail polish. S.T., S.W.

NEL - No. T.M.

NETA - A volley ball net. C.M.

NICLE - Nickle. T.M.

NIGASURA - Sling shot. S.T., S.W.

NIGUAS - Definitely not. S.W., C.M.

NI SOCA - Not a bit. T.M.

NIX - A term meaning absolutely "No." S.W.

NOCAUT - A knockout (boxing). M., L.A., S.W.

NO MAS NO - No way, man. T.M.

NONO (Arnoldo) - Nickname for Arnoldo. S.T., S.W.

NOQUIADO - To pass out during a drinking spree or binge. T.M.

NO TE CHIVELLES - Don't back up on your word, stick by your conviction. T.M., S.W.

NO TE RESVALES - Do not go astray. S.W.

NO TIENES HUEVOS - Does not have any courage at all. T.M., C.M.

NO VAYAS A REGARLA - Don't mess up. T.M.

NUBES (Andar en las nubes) - Day dreaming. T.M., S.W.

NUNE - Term meaning Junior. S.W.

O

OJALA - Hope so. T.M., S.W.

OJETE - A person who is considered extremely stingy in all respects; ass hole. S.T., S.W.

ONDA - A set pattern, contemporary movement and/or a style of living. T.M., S.W.

ORALE - Be careful, don't bug me. S.T., S.W.

OREJON (Pendejo) - Being made a fool of and/or having been taken for a fool. T.M.

ORITA - Now! T.M., S.W.

ORMI - Army. T.M., S.W.

ORUTAR - To burp. T.M., S.W.

OSICO - Mouth (animal); refers to persons who cuss a lot. T.M.

OSICONA - Bad mouthing. T.M.

P

PACHANGA - A party and/or a get-together with acquaintance. C.M., S.W.

PACHON - A hairy looking person. T.M., S.W.

PACHORO(A) - A slow poke, extremely easy-going person. T.M., M.

PACHUCO-EL CHUCO - A zoot-suiter. T.M., C.M., S.W.

PACOIMA - A "square." C.M.

PADROTE - A pimp. M., T.M.

PAINE - A comb and/or a brush (e.g., hair). T.M., S.W., M.

PAIPA - A pipe (water, gas). T.M., S.W.

PAJARIAR - To see, watch, and observe. T.M., S.W.

PAJUELA - A female who appreciates the companionship of males. (e.g., Coquette). T.M., S.W.

PAJUELAZO - Referring to a drink (e.g., a shot of liquor). T.M., S.W.

PAJUELIADO - Referring to a spanking (e.g., boy). T.M., S.W.

PAJUELIAR - To be walking and/or moving without any sense of direction (e.g., an entertainment mood). T.M., S.W.

PAL - Means "him" (e.g., him). T.M., N.M.

PALITOS - Clothespins. N.M.

PALLAMAS - Pajamas. T.M., N.M.

PALOMIA - The gang and/or peer group. S.T., T.M.

PALOMITAS - Pop corn. M., S.W.

PANALES - Baby diapers (e.g., cloth type). T.M., S.W.

PANCHO(A) - Lousy dressed. T.M., S.W.

PANDIARSE - To bend something (e.g., body, pipe, etc.). T.M., S.W.

PANOCHA - Mexican bread. T.M., M.

PANQUEQUE - Pancake. S.W.

PANSA - Stomach. T.M., S.W.

PANSONA - (derog. A pregnant female and/or pregnancy. T.M., S.W.

PANTALETAS - Female panties, underwear (e.g., garments). T.M., S.W.

PANTOCHA - A clown, impersonator and/or a devoted show-off. T.M.

PANZA MOJADA - An individual (e.g., Mexican from Mexico). T.M., S.W.

PAPACHAR - To consent and/or to encourage. T.M., S.W..

PAPALOTE - A kite. C.M., M.

PAPAS - Lies. T.M., M.

PAPELERO - A person who is considered a faker. T.M., S.W.

PAPERO - Pretender. T.M.

PAPIRO - The usual writing paper commonly used in the classrooms for seat work. T.M., U.O.

PAPITAS - Little white lies. T.M.

PAQUETE - An individual who desires and/or wants credit for anything accomplished. T.M., S.W.

PARADA - Backing up an individual in any circumstances and regardless of whatever happens. S.W.

PARA DONDE LA TIRAS - Where are you going. T.M., S.W.

PARED VERDE - Walgreen drug store. T.M., S.T.

PARIENTES - Relatives, kinfolks, and/or parents. T.M., S.W.

PARQUE - A public park, parking, and often considered to mean ammunition. T.M., S.W.

PARQUIADERO - Parking area (e.g., monthly rates). T.M., S.W.

PARRANDA - A group of people on a drinking spree (e.g., parties). T.M., S.W.

PARRANDIAR - To go and/or attend a drinking party with your intimate friends. T.M., S.W.

PARTAMONEDA - A billfold and/or a purse. T.M., S.W.

PARTERA - A midwife. T.M., M., S.W.

PASALE! - Enter! (e.g., come on in). T.M., S.W.

PASOTES - A good-looking male in all respects. T.M., S.W.

PASTILLA - Money (e.g., coins, dollars, etc.). T.M., S.W.

PATADA - Kick, thrill. T.M.

PATAS PARA DELANTE - To run backwards and/or retreat. S.W.

PATIADA - A woman and/or girl who has been around men (emotionally, socially and physically). T.M.

PEDO - An untrue fact or statement. T.M., S.W.

PEGOISTES - Tag along. T.M., S.W.

PELADO - A playboy; a sharp character and/or a lady's man. Also a member of the clan. (e.g., pimp, rascal, etc.) S.W.

PELARSE - To go, leave, and/or escape. T.M., S.W.

PELIONERO - A child adult who likes to fight. T.M., S.W.

PELISCAR - To pinch. (e.g., ears, cheeks, etc.) T.M., S.W.

PELOTA - To be really in love. T.M.

PELUQUERO - A barber and/or a person who gambles and wins. T.M.

PENCO - A child born out of wedlock. T.M., M., S.W.

PENDEJADA - To do something stupid and/or uncalled for. T.M., S.W., L.A.

PENDEJIAR - To foul up, make a mistake. S.T., S.W.

PENDEJO - Stupid. S.W.

PENITENCIA - A penitentiary, detention center, prison. T.M., S.W.

PEPE (Jose) - Nickname for Jose and/or Joe. T.M., S.W.

PEPENA - The left-overs after a harvest (e.g., cotton crop). S.T., S.W.

PERICA - Radio. S.W.

PERILLA - A sty (e.g., tumor on eyelid). S.T., S.W.

PERRICO - A talkative individual. S.T., S.W.

PERRO CALLIENTE - A Hot Dog. S.W.

PERUSQUIA - An individual who loves to drink alcoholic beverages. T.M.

PESUDO - A wealthy person. T.M.

PESUNA - The feet and/or foot. T.M.

PETATIARSE - To die. S.T., S.W.

PICALE! - Go ahed! (e.g., move forward). S.T., S.W.

PICALE LA CRESTA - Make him mad. S.T.

PICA OJOS - An individual and/or person who takes advantage of another person. T.M.

PICAR - To eat very little (e.g., food). S.T., S.W.

PICHAR - To pitch (e.g., baseball pitcher). S.T., S.W.

PICHER - A baseball pitcher. T.M, S.W.

PICHICATE - A stingy individual (e.g., parasite). T.M., S.W.

PICHON - An easy make. T.M.

PICHONIAR - To pet. T.M.

PICLE - A pickle. S.T., S.W.

PICO - A big mouth or just a frontage of something that is not true. T.M.

PICON - A trouble maker. T.M., S.W.

PICOTIAR - To eat a small amount of food (e.g., choice of particular food). T.M., S.W.

PIEDRA - A stingy character or uncooperative person when dealing monetary factors. T.M., S.W.

PILMAMA - A baby sitter or a person who stays home to care for children. T.M., M.

PILOTIAR - To drive a car and/or automobile. S.T.

PIMIENTITO - Real small person. S.W.

PINCHE - A stingy person in terms of material items and/or money. T.M.

PINCHES - Clothes pins (P.R.). Stingy person (derog.). P.R., T.M., S.W.

PINGA - A devilish type of female, tricky, odd. (T.M., C.M.

PINGAS - A group of females who are considered devilish. T.M., C.M.

PINGO - A devilish type of male, tricky, odd. T.M., C.M.

PINTATE - To beat it, to move or to get away. T.M., S.W.

PINTO - A convict. S.W.

PIOJO - A person who tags along with a crowd. S.T.

PIPA - A smoking pipe. S.T., S.W.

PIPIRIN - Snack, lunch, food. T.M., S.W.

PIQUETIAR - To picket and/or boycott. T.T., S.W.

PIQUINIC - A picnic. S.T., S.W.

PIRUJA - A sly gal. S.T.

PIRUJO - A sly guy. S.T.

PISON - To be stepped on (e.g., by a foot). T.M., S.W.

PISPORRIA - A bump on the head. S.T., S.W.

PISTIARSE - An individual who has drunk alcoholic beverages. S.T., S.W.

PISTO - Any alcoholic beverage, such as beer, wine, and hard liquor. T.M., S.W.

PISTONIAR - An individual who does complete his verbal expression due to an uncertain factor. T.M., S.W.

PIYIDO - A short, brief scream. S.T., S.W.

PIZCA - A harvest (e.g., cotton, fruits). T.M., S.W.

PLANCHAR OREJA - An individual who is going to bed. T.M., S.W.

PLANTADO - A male who has been stood-up by a female (normally a date). S.T., S.W.

PLASTA - Hair oil and/or greasy. T.M., S.W.

PLATO - Record. S.W., C.M.

PLEBE - Normally utilized in New Mexico which refers to the people of the area or group. Toasi, N.M.

PLUGES - Spark plugs. T.M., S.W.

PLUJIAR - To plunge. S.T., S.W.

PLUMA - A woman who is considered loose in nature, not married and who goes around with married and/or unmarried males; prostitute. S.W., T.M.

PONCHO - A Chicano born in the U.S. M., T.M.

POCHOLOGICO - Monterrey Tech. S.T., T.M.

POLA (Leopolda) - Nickname for Leopold. T.M., S.W.

POMPA - A water pump. S.T., S.W.

PONCHAR - To strike, punch and/or hit someont physically. T.M., S.W.

PONES GORO - You bore me. S.W., T.M.

PONSELO - Sock it to him and/or her. S.W., T.M.

PONTE AL ALVA - Be alert. T.M.

POPE - Puppy (e.g., dog). T.M., S.W.

POQUIAR - To play poker. S.W.

PORE - Party. T.M., S.W.

POSO - Getting after an item (eg., to work, play, etc.). T.M., S.W.

POSTE - Tall, skinny guy and/or girl. S.W.

POSTERO - An American hillbilly (Anglo). (derog.) T.M.

PRECULA - Pre-cooler apparatus for vegetables. S.W.

PRENDER - To get hooked on the drug habit. S.W.

PRENDIDO - To be hooked on something. S.T., S.W.

PRIETA - Often referring to one's woman a wife. S.T.

PUCHAR - To push. T.M., S.W.

PUCHI! - A bad smell (e.g., odor). S.T., S.W.

PUEBLUCHO - A small town. T.M., S.W.

PUELA - A frying pan (commonly used in northern New Mexico). N.M.

PUL - Influence (e.g., pull). S.T., S.W.

PULIAR - To influence. T.M., S.W.

PULMAN - Pullman (e.g., train).

PUNTA - The point of a pencil, pen, etc. T.M., M., S.W.

PUNTADA - A hint. S.T., S.W.

PUNTIAS - Tacks. N.M., S.W.

PURITITO - The whole truth and nothing but the truth. T.M., S.W.

PURO PEDO - Hog wash and/or not really serious. T.M., S.W.

PUSO GORRO - A certain person and/or a group of people who are always harrassing someone. S.T., T.M.

Q

QUADRAR - To like, appreciate a specific person. T.M., S.W.

QUARTERON - A mulato-half Spanish Black. T.M., S.W.

QUARTIADO - A half-breed and/or a person who is actually afraid. T.M., S.W.

QUE AGUANTE - What strength, tolerance. T.M., S.W.

QUECHAR - To catch and/or to cash a check. (e.g., baseball or a check, money) T.M., S.T.

QUECHER - A baseball catcher (baseball). S.T., S.W.

QUEIQUE - A cake and/or pastry. T.M., S.W.

QUELITE - A common weed in South Texas, etc. T.M., S.W., M.

QUEMADO - A person who is not trustworthy. S.W.

QUEMAR - To blacklist an individual for some of his personal actions or beliefs. T.M., S.W.

QUENCA - Head, skull. T.M.

QUEQUE - A new Mexican expression meaning pastry. N.M., S.W.

QUERMES - A church group function (e.g., celebration, food games, etc.). S.T., S.W.

QUE SUAVE - That's good and/or a verbal approval of something significant. T.M., S.W.

QUIENTEMANDA - An old saying such as "I told you so." T.M., M.

QUINCE ABRILES - Fifteen years old. M., T.M., S.W.

QUINDER - Kindergarten. S.T., S.W.

QUIRA - An American quarter-twenty-five cents. T.M., S.W.

QUIRE - A kitty (e.g., cat, etc.). S.T., S.W.

QUISAS - Girls and/or gals. T.M., S.W.

R

RADIODERIA - A radiator. T.M, S.W.

RAFE - Female nickname for Rafaela. T.M., S.W., S.T.

RAITIAR - To ride. T.M.

RAJO - Backed out on his word; chopping wood. T.M., S.W.

RAJON - Stool Pidgeon; person who squeals on another person. T.M., S.W.

RALEYA - A group of people in particular. M., S.W.

RAMFLA - Auto. T.M.

RAQUETA - A racket such as a dope racket. T.M., S.W.

RAQUETERO - Hoodlum. T.M., S.W.

RASCUACHE - A good-for-nothing character. T.M., S.W.

RASPA - Trash, scum (e.g., people). T.M., S.W.

RASPON - A scratch. S.T., S.W.

RATONADA - A messy and dirty place. T.M., S.W.

RAYA - Daily, weekly and monthly wages. S.T., S.W.

RAYADOR - A radiator. S.T., S.W., L.A.

RAYAR - To curse. S.W.

RAYON - Rayon (e.g., cloth material). T.M., N.M.

RAZA - Chicano, Mexican, Mexican-American, Spanish-American, Cuban, Puerto Rican (e.g., race). S.T., M., S.W.

REAJUSTE - A period of readjustment. (e.g., job, sports, marriage, etc.) T.M., M., S.W.

REATAZO - A physical blow. S.T., S.W.

REBATE - To jump ahead of time an uncalled selfish movement to benefit one's self. T.M.

REBOTAR - To be rejected by a group. S.T., S.W.

RECARGARSELA - To boast about your accomplishment. S.T., S.W.

RECORTAR - To be laid off. (e.g., job) S.T., S.W.

REDITIRSE - To melt. (e.g., Snow Cone, ice cream cone) S.T., S.W.

REFINAR - To eat. T.M., S.W.

REGARLA - An individual who makes a statement or does something unusual that promotes a problem. T.M., S.W.

RELAJAR - To scold, bawl out, to humiliate. T.M., S.W.

RELIS - To be discharged and/or dismissed. (e.g., military service, prison, etc.) T.M., M., S.W.

RELAJE - Disgrace, ridicule. T.M., S.W.

REMPLE - An automobile. S.T., S.W.

REPELIDO - A constant argument and/or discussion. T.M., S.W.

REPETIR - To burp. T.M., S.W.

REQUE - A car wreck. T.M., S.W.

RESBALON - A slick and shrewd male. T.M., S.W.

RESBALONA - A teaser; a slick person, usually a woman (resbalona). T.M., S.W.

RESTA - Restaurant. T.M., M.

RETRA - Picture. T.M., M., S.W.

REVERSA - Reverse gear. (e.g., car). S.T., S.W.

REZONGAR - To object about something. T.M., S.W.

RIELES - Female legs. T.M., S.W.

RIFARSE - To be a stand-out. (e.g., football star scoring most of the points) S.T., S.W.

RILEY - Track relay (e.g., game, sports). T.M., S.W.

RIN - A rim (e.g., part of a car). S.T., S.W.

RINCHE - Texas Ranger. T.M., S.W.

RISIONADA - An act that causes a laughter. T.M., S.W.

RODILLA - A person considered one's rival in love and/or game. T.M.

ROL - A car. T.M., S.W.

ROLA - A song. T.M., S.W.

ROLANTE - A car (e.g., regional speech variants for the word automobile). S.T., C.M., S.W.

ROLAR - To go to sleep. T.M.

ROLAS - Songs. T.M., S.W.

ROLE - A different regional dialect meaning car. T.M., C.M., S.W.

ROLIAR - To physically assault and commit a robbery. S.W.

RONDARSE - To hang out. T.M.

ROQUIROL - An exotic American dance, Rock 'n' Roll. L.A., M.

ROST - A roast. T.M., S.W.

RUCA - Girl and or girl friend. T.M., S.W.

RUCAILA(O) - An elderly person. T.M., S.W.

RUCO - Husband, man boy friend and/or an old man. T.M., S.W.

RUEDA DE SAN MIGUAL - A game for children (e.g., specially among Chicanos). T.M., S.W.

RUFO - Freight train. C.M.

RUINA - Bad luck. T.M., S.W.

RULA - Ruler. T.M.

RUSCA (Pinche) - Stingy. T.M.

S

SABANAS PAQUETES DE HILO - What I told you. N.M., Taosisy.

SACALE! - Pencil sharpener (e.g., manual). T.M., S.W.

SACATE - Get out of here, get off my back. T.M., S.W.

SACATE TU - You get out. T.M., S.W., N.M.

SACATIAR - A physical struggle, to shake up a person. T.M., S.W.

SAFADO - He's out of his mind. T.M., M., S.W.

SAFIS - An excuse made by a person who has just made an error. T.M., M., S.W.

SAINIAR - To sign (e.g., contract). T.M., S.W.

SAL - Extremely bad luck. T.M., S.W.

SALE - Let's go. T.M., S.W.

SALIRLE O SEGUIRLE DE FRENTE - Going all the way out in the use of narcotics and becoming a main liner as soon as possible while using stolen money and other sources to obtain money. T.M., S.W.

SALADO - The unfortunate one, bad luck. T.M.

SAN ANTO - San Antonio, Texas. T.M., S.W.

SANCHO - A regular playboy that concentrates on married women. T.M., M.

SANGRE - Blood and/or a term meaning "No." S.W., C.M.

SANGRE DE CHANGO - A medication meaning iodine and/or mecurochrome.

SANGRON - Hateful. T.M., S.W.

SARDO - An Army Sergeant (non-commissioned officer). S.W., S.T., M.

SATIRO - A senile gentleman, elderly person. M., T.M.

SE AJILO - He took off walking. T.M., M., S.W.

SE AMACANO - An individual who refuses to move. T.M., S.W.

SEA POR DIOS - That's the way God wants it to be. T.M., S.W.

SE FLOTA UNA - Drank a beer. T.M., S.W.

SE HULLO - Took off and got married. T.M., S.W., M.

SE LA PINTO - He took off. T.M., S.W.

SE LE FUE LA ONDA - A peron show is conversing normally then changes his subject suddenly. T.M., S.W.

SE MANDO - Got carried away and/or took advantage of. T.M., S.W.

SEMBLANTIAR - A sense of observation to find out the intentions of people. T.M., S.W.

SENSEN - A Chicano game played with marbles. T.M., M., S.W.

SERENATIAR - To give someone a serenade. T.M., S.W.

SESONAN - Sniff glue. T.M., S.W.

SESOS - Brain. T.M., S.W.

SESUMIO - An individual who owes money and/or favors. T.M., S.W.

SETIAR - To set one's hair (e.g., Beauty Shop). T.M., S.W.

SE VOLARON LAS COSAS - Things were stolen, to steal. T.M., S.W., M.

SIGELE! - Sic 'em (e.g., an expression made by some Chicanos). T.M., S.W.

SILABARIO - Yes (e.g., an affirmative answer). T.M., S.W.

SIMON - Yes. T.M., S.W.

SINC - A sink (e.g., to wash dishes). T.M., S.W.

SIROL - Yes. T.M., S.W.·

SISTA - Sister (e.g., like brother). T.M., S.W.

SNOBISMO - Snob. M., S.W.

SOBADOR - Person who rubs parts of the body for healing purposes. T.M., M.

SOBRES - Overshoes. N.M., S.W.

SODONGA - Soda water. C.M., M.

SOFACIAR - To be lying down on a sofa. T.M., S.W.

SOFOQUE - To bawl out someone. T.M., S.W.

SOKET - Socket. M., S.W.

SOLDAR - To weld and/or to solder. T.M., S.W.

SONAJIAR - To punish a child by a spanking. T.M., S.W.

SONAR - A term meaning to strike an individual physically. T.M., S.W.

SONGAS - Songs. C.M., S.W., S.T.

SONSIAR - To joke around and/or to fool around as a joker of a party. T.M., S.W.

SONSO - Refers to a person that anybody can make a fool of. T.M., S.W.

SOPLADO - A heavy-set individual, fat. T.M., M.

SOPLON - Being bawled out and/or getting after someone. T.M., S.W.

STEPIAR - A step (e.g., firm footstep). T.M., S.W.

SUATO(A) - Psycho; in touch with reality. T.M., S.W.

SUAVE - Easy and/or good. T.M., S.W.

SUELAZO - To slip down on the floor. (e.g., flat on floor). T.M., S.W.

71

SUERTUDO - Very fortunate person; a lucky individual. T.M., S.W.

SUICHE - A light switch (e.g., button). T.M., S.W.

SUMBAR - Concerns an individual who is extremely good at anything (e.g., sports, games, food). T.M., S.W.

SU MERCED - Yes, sir. M., N.M., 16th century Spanish.

SURA - Silly, boring and/or a person who is not well-liked. T.M., C.M., S.W.

SWEE-CHI - Light switch. M., S.W.

SWETER - Sweater. S.W., M., S.T.

SWINGULAR - Selling sugar content or other substitutes to young and unexperienced joy poppers. S.W., T.M.

T

TABAQUIADO - To smoke and/or to be smoking. T.M., S.W.

TABIQUE - Jail; place of detention for prisoners and correctional institution. T.M., S.W.

TABIRO - A jail. T.M., S.W.

TACONASO - A Chicano dance popular in northern Mexico and Texas. T.M., M.

TACUCHO - A dress suit compared to a tuxedo. T.M., M., S.W.

TAIPIADOR(A) - An individual who types for living. T.M., S.W.

TAIPIAR - To type (e.g., typewriter). T.M., S.W.

TALACHE - A pick (e.g., garden tool, etc.). T.M., S.W.

TALONIAR - To hustle and/or push one's belief in order to secure one's wish. T.M.

TAMOB - Jail; detention center and correctional institution. T.M., S.W.

TAMBORETIADO - A tired individual after a fight and/or after work. T.M., S.W.

TAMBORETIAR - To physically whip someone. T.M., S.W.

TANATES - A person who has a strong character. S.W.

TANDO - A straight and sturdy individual. T.M., S.W.

TANGO - A town and/or a city. T.M.

TAPADO(A) - Naive, ignorant, and narrow-minded individual. T.M., S.W.

TAPIO - A well-known Chicano artist in Edinburg, Texas. S.T., M.

TAQUACHITO - A typical Chicano dance considered a polka. T.M.

TARANTULA - A hairy-looking individual. T.M.

TARIS - A detention center jail (e.g., regional). T.M., S.W.

TARLANGO - A hat and/or a sombrero. T.M., S.W.

TARTANA - An old vehicle (e.g., car). T.M., S.W.

TARUGO - Stupid, dumb and silly. T.M., S.W.

TASAJIAR - To cut, slice (e.g., meat, etc.). T.M., S.W.

TASCALCUAN - An insect, cockroach. T.M., S.W.

TASON - A hard-headed individual with no common sense. T.M.

TAYAS - Automobile tires. S.W.

TAYUDO - An individual considered stubborn and strong in strength. T.M., M., S.W.

TAXA - A tax (e.g., on goods). T.M., S.W.

TECATO - Heroin user. T.M., S.W.

TECLA - Cigarette stub or butt; out of tune with time. T.M., S.W.

TECORUCHO - A small, old house. T.M., S.W.

TECOLOTE - An underpaid, self-proclaimed policeman, and/or night watchman along the Mexican side of the border. M., T.M.

TEIPIAR - To seal, tape a package. T.M, S.W.

TEJON - Real short guy, Texas. S.W.

TELE - A baby's feeding bottle; female breast. T.M., S.W.

TELEFONZAO - A telephone call. T.M., S.W.

TENDAJERO - A store owner (e.g., any type). T.M., S.W.

TENDAJO - A food store (e.g., Garcia's Food Store, Foodland, H.E.B.). T.M., S.W.

TENDIDO - To stretch out; to lay out or flatten on one's back. T.M.

TENER FUCHI - To be afraid. T.M.

TENIDO - To rely on; to depend on someone in particular. T.M.

TENISTA - A tennis player. T.M., S.W.

TE PICARON LOS OJOS - They made a fool out of you. T.M., S.W.

TE PICAS - A person who is jealous of someone who has done some extraordinary deeds. S.W.

TE RALLASTES - An individual who has hit the jackpot and/or has accomplished a rewarding task. T.M., S.W.

TERQUIAR - To be persistent; to keep on trying. T.M.

TERREGAL - Whirlwind (e.g., dirt, etc.). T.M., S.W.

TERREMOTE - Dirt clod, hard chunky piece of dirt. T.M., S.W.

TE SALISTES - You're out of line, an uncalled for remark. T.M., S.W.

TESTADOR - An examiner, tester. T.M., S.W.

TIATRO - A theatre (e.g., movies). S.T., S.W.

TICHAR - To teach (e.g., classroom instructions). T.M., S.W.

TICURUCHO - An old shack, one or two room house. T.M., S.W.

TILDILLO - A specific bird of a specific region (e.g., sparrow, blackbirds, etc.). T.M., N.M., S.W.

TILICHES - Old furniture, bags and/or luggage. T.M., S.W.

TILTIAR - To tilt (e.g., an object). T.M., S.W.

TINACO - A city water tower (storage) from which the population drinks. T.M., M., S.W.

TINNER - Thinner. M., S.W.

TINTO - A name given by some Chicanos to Blacks (derog.). TEX•Mex, T.M.

TIO TACO - A Mexican-American "Uncle Tom" as determined by the contemporary youth movement of Chicanos. S.W.

TIRACHO - Afro-American, Black and or Negro. T.M., S.W.

TIRADO - Wearing lousy clothes. T.M.

TIRA LA MASA - Going to the bathroom to dispose of one's waste. T.M.

TIRAR A LEON - To completely ignore an individual by any means. T.M., S.W.

TIRAR AL LOCO - To ignore someone. T.M.

TIRAR CHANCLA - To dance. T.M., S.W.

TIRAR A LUCAS - To completely avoid and/or ignore an individual for specific reasons. T.M., S.W.

TIRAR VONQUE - To go to sleep. T.M.

TIRON - Considered a female who normally is messing around with one in particular. S.W.

TIRONTIANDO - A physical bombardment and/or by means of weapons such as shooting up a place. T.M., S.W.

TITA - Nickname for Theresa. T.M., S.W.

TITO - Nickname for Hector. T.M., S.W.

TIZON - An individual with a dark complexion, not necessarily pertaining to a racial segment. T.M., S.W.

TOCADISCOS - A combination of a radio and record player (e.g., phonograph and radio). T.M., S.W.

TOFUDO - Tough, rough. T.M., S.W.

TOMARLE EL PELO - To take advantage of any given situation in order to achieve a set goal. T.M., S.W.

TOMATIAR - To bombard verbally an individual after his discussion (e.g., to critique). T.M., S.W.

TOMATERA - A female tomato picker. T.M., S.W.

TONINA JACKSON - A heavy-set person. T.M., M.

TONTARRIAJE - Group of persons who are not aware of what happens (e.g., lack of pertinent knowledge). T.M., S.W.

TOPO - A person considered stupid, unintelligent. S.W.

TOQUE - To inhale a marijuana cigarette. T.M., S.W.

TORCER - To arrest; to die and/or pass away or an easy set up to be picked up by the police. T.M., S.W.

TORCHA - Matches. S.W.

TORCIDO - A person who has been apprehended by the law; angry-looking individual. T.M., S.W.

TORIQUIAR - To speak. T.M., S.W.

TORTIAR - To clap hands and/or an individual who has been telling fables. T.M., S.W.

TOSTON - Half dollar (e.g., fifty cent piece). T.M., S.W.

TOTACHA - A unique method of communication in a bilingual form utilized by Chicanos. T.M., S.W.

TOTACHAR - To speak one of the Chicano regional speech variants (e.g., Calo, Tex-Mex). T.M., S.W.

TRABUSCA - A glutton. C.M.

TRACALADA - A commotion, loud noise. T.M., S.W.

TRACOS - Shoes. T.M., S.W.

TRAGADO - A heavy eater (food; heavy or huge appetite). T.M., S.W.

TRAGON - A heavy eater, a person who eats a lot. T.M., S.W.

TRAMADOS - Pants. T.M., S.W.

TRAMPIAR - To trap animals (e.g., cages, etc.). T.M., S.W.

TRANCASOS - A physical blow-up by means of a fist fight. T.M., S.W.

TRAPOS - Clothes. T.M., S.W.

TRAQUIADO - Worn out individual; tired and beyond the physical or mental repair stage. T.M.

TRASAMBRIDO - Hopeless, malnutrition, and hungry-looking individual. T.M.

TRAZAS - A set pattern of dressing-behavior and/or a particular physical sight of an individual. T.M.

TREILA - A trailer (e.g., commercial truck). T.M., S.W.

TRILAZO - A thrill (e.g., celebration, etc.). T.M., S.W.

TRINCHE - A fork (e.g., to eat food). T.M., S.W.

TRINKETE - A trick or a piece of junk. T.M.

TRIPA - Water hose or skinny fellow. S.W.

TRIPON - A youngster below the age of ten. T.M., S.W.

TROCA - A truck. T.M.

TROCHES MOCHIS - Doing something unusual without a sense of direction. T.M.

TROLA - Match, lighter. T.M., S.W.

TROLIS - An individual considered abnormal and/or a person who is not functioning to his full caPACITY. T.M.

TROMPA - The mouth lips of a human being or a top. T.M., S.W.

TROMPUDO - Big lips. T.M., S.W.

TROMPEZAR - To trip over (e.g., fall down). T.M., S.W.

TROMPO - A slick-sturdy dancer and/or a top (game). T.M., S.W.

TROMPUDO - Big lips. T.M., S.W.

TORNARLA - To shoot; put away and/or legally dispose of a particular individual by some unusual means. T.M.

TROQUERO - A truck driver. T.M., S.W.

TROSTIAR - To trust a person. T.M., S.W.

TRUCHA - An alert person in any given situation. T.M., S.W.

TRUCHON - A sly and alert individual in a given situation. T.M., S.W.

TRUENOS - Thunderstorm. T.M., S.W.

TRUJE - I brought. S.W., M.

TUNICO - Two American nickles. S.W., T.M.

U

ULES - Soles. S.W.

UNA BARRA - A drinking bar. T.M., S.W.

UNA CACHUCHA - Also one capsule of heroin. S.W.

UNA CHORA - A cigarette butt. T.M., S.W.

UNA CURVIA - To beat around and/or avoid a particular issue. T.M.

UNA LISTA - A list referring to a specific name and/or names. T.M.

UNA MONA - A doll. S.W.

UNA PLUMA - A prostitute. S.W.

UNA TROLA - A match to light up a cigarette. T.M., S.W.

UNA VIENTE - Police utilizing one addict against another to inform or make a buy from. S.W.

UN AVENTON - A lift; a push. T.M., S.W.

UN BERRINCHE - Temper, tantrum. T.M., S.W.

UN FINO - A queer and/or a queen (homosexual). S.W.

UN GRAMO - One gram of heroin. S.W.

UN MANCHADO - An individual with a police record. S.W.

UN RAJETAS - A stool pigeon, and/or a squealer turncoat in the Barrio. T.M.

UN TALON - Half a dollar and/or fifty cents. T.M., S.W.

UN TAYUDO - An old man. S.W.

UN YESCO - A dope addict, normally a user of marijuana. T.M., S.W.

V

VACILAR - To fool around, flirt. T.M.

VAGONERO - Railroad worker (e.g., one that hooks cars). T.M., S.W.

VALAS - Loose women, flirt, teaser. T.M., S.W.

VALER SOQUETE - An unworthy individual. T.M., S.W.

VAMOS AL GUARACHASO - Let's go dancing. T.M.

VAMOS AL MONO - Let's to the theater or movie. T.M., S.W.

VAMPIRO - An individual considered a blood-thirsty character. T.M., S.W.

VENADO - A square. S.W.

VENTO - Nickname for Ventura. S.T.

VERDOLAGAS - Green, inexperienced. S.W.

VERIGUATA - An argument, disagreement and/or a loud mass confusion. T.M., S.W.

VIDRIOS - Eye glasses, shades, and/or bifocals. S.W.

VIROLES - Beans. S.W.

VIRUELA LOCA - Chickenpox. T.M., S.W., M.

VIRULO - An eye. T.M., S.W.

VITROLA - An old phonograph. T.M., S.W., N.M.

VOLANDO - To walk or go in a hurry. T.M.

VOLARON LAS TAPAS - Blew his top in anger. T.M.

W

WELDIARDO - Welder. T.M.

WIFA - An espouse and/or a wife. T.M., S.W., C.M.

WIZA - A woman and/or a girl friend. T.M., C.M., S.W.

WAUGUA - Bus. P.R., U.S.

X

Y

YA ESTUFAS - That's enough. T.M., S.W.

YA NO LA MUELAS - Do not harm him, let him be. T.M., S.W.

YARDA - A yard (e.g., grass, etc.). T.M., S.W.

YEC - A car jack. T.M., S.W.

YENO - Contented. T.M.

YERBA BUENA - Coming from good breed and/or marijuana. T.M.

YERBERO - Herbalist. T.M., M., S.W.

YES - Jazz (e.g., type of music). T.M., S.W.

YIN - Cotton gin. T.M., S.W.

YIPE - An Army jeep. T.M., S.T., S.W.

YIRA - Jitterbug (e.g., type of dance). T.M., S.W.
YOGAS - Me, d- T.M.
YOMPA - Jumper (dress), a cowboy jumper. T.M., S.W.
YONCA - A means of transportation, a bicycle. T.M.
YONQUE or YONKE - Junk, junk yard. T.M.

Z

ZAFADO - Crazy, out of his head, stupid. T.M., S.W.
ZAFO - An expression used to be excused from a game (e.g., if a person is about to lose). T.M., S.W.
ZAMBUTIER - To get further in debt. T.M., S.W.
ZAPATOS - Putting down another person. T.M., S.W.
ZAPOS - Shoes. S.W.
ZIGSAQUIAR - To zig-zag, move around. T.M., S.W.
ZOQUETE - Mud. T.M., S.W.
ZOQUETOSO - Muddy. T.M., S.W.
ZUMBARSE - To eat something quickly without being noticed. T.M., S.W.
ZURDARZO - A left handed blow (e.g., punch). T.M., S.W.

Chicano-Hispano Americano
Phrases
(Totacha Phraseology)

Chicano Hispano Dialect (Totacha) Standard English.

El man esta en la house. The man is in the house.

Americans viven en buenas houses. Americans live in good houses.

Los cantones de los Chicanos are clean. The Chicano homes are clean.

Los chucos son "cool guys." The zoot-suiters are cool guys.

La placa are los friends de los "Chucos." The Policemen are the friends of the zoot-suiters.

Los Chicanitos have to taloniar mas hard que los anglos. The Chicanitos have to work harder than the Anglos.

Friends son los que dan la hand a others. Friends are those that lend their hands to others.

Mr. Allen es un man que tiene un job muy important. Mr. Allen is a man who has a very important job.

La chavala is very bonita. The girl is very pretty.

Los cuetes are bastante dangerous. The guns are very dangerous.

The Policemen gave los Chavalos unos tickets. The Policeman gave the guys some tickets.

Some people believe que todos semos lazy en la escuela. Some people believe that most of us are lazy in school.

Los Ricos se fueron a rolar in good beds. The rich went to bed in good beds.

Mi jefita lives en el state of Texas. My mother lives in Texas.

Voltaire digo one time que el pensaba that todos vivian en un society. Voltaire once said that he thought that all of us lived in one society.

We want to go a chancliar a la nite. We want to go dancing tonight.

Los Mayates are the cuates of the Chicanos. The Blacks are the brothers of the Chicanos.

We have buenos Profe's en las schools. We have good teachers in our schools.

Jacinto Trevino College is the primer Colejio Chicano en los United States. Jacinto Trevino College is the first Chicano College in the U.S.A.

El pinto is a persona que has been en la Pinta. The convict is a person who has been in a correctional institution.

The Capitan is often llamado el capirucho by Chicanos. The Capitan is often called a Capitan by Chicanos.

The Agringado is often called un Bendido. The Americanized Chicano is often called a sell-out.

Some Chicanos son muy talented. Some Chicanos are extremely talented.

Chicanos necesitan un buena parada en nuestros colleges. Chicanos need a break in our colleges.

On account of the Grifa many Chicanos have been entavicados. On account of marijuana many Chicanos have been jailed.

Los calcos are often muy caros. The shoes are often very expensive.

The State of Califa les da papiro a los students. The State of California gives out paper to their students.

The students se mira muy malancones. The students look extremely sick.

Todos tenemos lot of teles en our casas. We have many televisions in our homes.

The feria es muy importante in the lives of la gente. Money is very important in the lives of the people.

I want un hot dog. I want a hot dog.

We have un box spring en our cama. We have a box spring in our bed.

La Casa de los Hotcakes. The House of Pancakes.

Ay te guacho tomorrow. I'll see you tomorrow.

El Principal said "Simon" to the students. The Principal said "Yes" to the students.

They made a trinquete to my jefita en la store. They played a trick on my mother at the store.

La vida es algo muy pretty. The life is something very pretty.

Jim Pluckett es un Chicano muy famous. Jim Puckett is a famous Chicano.

My carucha is not a ford, pero un Cadillac. My car is not a Ford, but a Cadillac.

Our padres quieren the best para their chamacos. Our parents want the best for their children.

Chale, those huercos are O.K. That's not right, those guys are O.K.

Avientalo a loco when he comes in. Just ignore him when he comes in.

That guy is taking pingas very often. That guy is taking pills very often.

Our jefitos are muy calmados today. Our parents are very calm today.

El Mercado de Paperbacks. The Paperback Market.

The Guachiman workes en el Highland Mall. The Watchman works at the Highland Mall.

Los Chopinsen are grande. The Shopping Centers are big.

Las schools teach clase bilingues. The schools teach bilingual classes.

The Bilingual Teachers en Tejas are los mas qualified en los United States. The Bilingual Teachers in Texas are the most qualified in the United States.

Los Methods bilingues are very importantes. The Bilingual Methods are very important.

Los Consultants en las conferencias educativas drink muchos jaibols. The Consultants in the educational conferences drink lots of highballs.

Unos Educators Mejigo Americanos tend to olvidar that los Chicanitos have educational problems. Some Mexican-American educators tend to forget that young Mexican-Americans have educational problems.

Quiero que saqen sus pencils y papers para escribir una letter. I want you all to take out your pencils and paper to write a letter.

Los Professors estan dando clases bilingues. The Professors are offering bilingual classes.

La cultura del Mejico Americano es unique. The Mexican-American culture is unique.

Los Spanish-speaking chamacos are not bilingual pero trilingual. The Spanish-speaking children are not bilingual but trilingual.

Dr. Ballesteros hacido named el Dean de un Colegio en California. Dr. Ballesteros has been named Dean of a School in California.

La Profesora Anna Scala Cooney se va a live en el estado de Vermont. The Professor Anna Scala Cooney has gone to live in the state of Vermont.

Kenito se parece as su Uncle Ruben Canche. Kenito looks like his Uncle Ruben Canche.

Anna Cooney vuelve para su chante in Texas. Anna Cooney returns to her home in Texas.

La Jura is waiting a los borachos. The Police is waiting for the drunkards.

Tomas Cooney es un bato muy sport. Tom Cooney is a good sport.

Los Mexican-Americans son muy brave en Viet Nam. The Mexican-Americans are extremely brave in Viet Nam.

Bibliography

Adkins, P. G. "Language Acquisition and Dialecticism." **TESL Reporter,** Volume IV, No. I, Fall, 1970.

Alba, Victor. **The Mexicans.** United States of America: Frederick A. Praeger, 1967. An Interpretation of the Mexicans and Their Way of Life.

Andersson, Theodore, Boyer, Mildred. **Bilingual Schooling in the United States.** Southwest Educational Development Laboratory, Austin, Texas. January, 1970. Volumes I and II.

Barker, George C. "Social Function of Language in a Mexican American Community." **Acta Americana,** Volume V, No. III, 1947.

Bernal, Ignacio. **3000 Years of Art and Life in Mexico.** N.Y.: Harry N. Abrams, Incorporated. Art and Life dating back to three thousand years are superbly displayed in the National Museum of Anthrology in Capultepec Park, Mexico City. Pictures of this art and life are displayed in this book.

Bernstein, Basil. "Bernstein's Study of Social Class and Language." **Education, Economy, and Society.** N.Y.: Free Press of Glencoe Incorporated, 1962.

Carter, Thomas P. **Mexican Americans in School: A History of Education Neglect.** United States: Connecticut Printers, Incorporated, 1970. Presents a picture of the education and schooling of Mexican Americans.

Davis, Alba L. "Social Dialects and Social Change." **The Instructor.** Volume 75, pp. 93 +, March, 1966.

Day, Mark. **Forty Acres: Cesar Chavez and the Farm Workers.** New York, N.Y.: Praeger Publishers, 1971. Mark Days' vivid account of his experiences in fighting for the rights of the farm workers along with Cesar Chavez.

Green, William D. "Language and the Culturally Different" **English Journal.** Volume 54, pp. 724-, November, 1965.

Haugen, Einar. Term defined by, 7-9. **Bilingual Schooling in the United States.** Southwest Educational Development Laboratory, Austin, Texas, 1970. Volume 1. Authors, T. Andersson and M. Boyer.

Heller, Celia. **Mexican American Youth: Forgotten Youth at the Crossroad.** Random House, 1966. A Study of Mexican American Youth.

Horne, Elliot. **Hiptionary,** N.Y., Simon and Schuster, 1963. **Education Across Culture.** Miles V. Zintz. William C. Brown Book Company, Iowa, 1965.

"Language Problems for the Disadvantaged," **NCTE Task Force on Teaching English to the Disadvantaged.** Champaign, Illinois: NCTE: 1965.

Loflin, Marcin D. "A Teaching Problem in Non-Standard Negro English." **English Journal,** Volume 56, pp. 1312-1314, December, 1967.

Manuel, Hershel T., Spanish Speaking Children in the Southwest. University of Texas Press, Austin, 1965.

McCallum, George. Idiom Drills: For Student of English as a Second Language. Thomas Y. Crowell Company, Incorporated, 1970.

McDavid, Raven I. Austin, William M., Research found in **NCTE, Task Force on Teaching English to the Disadvantaged.** Champaign, Illinois: NCTE, 1965.

McWilliams, Carey. **North From Mexico.** Greenwood Press, N.Y., 1968.

Mexican-American in the United States: **A Reader.** Schenkman Publishing Company, Incorporated, Massachusetts, 1970.

Sanchez, George I. **Forgotten People: A Study of New Mexicans.** Albuquerque: Calvin Horn Pub. Incorporated, 1970. It's about exactly what the title implies.

Steiner, Stan. **La Raza,** Harper and Rowe Publishers, N.Y., 1968.

Vasquez, Librado Keno. An Experimental Pilot Bilingual Model School for Transient Mexican American Students. Xerox Corporation, Ann Arbor, Michigan, 1970.

Wentworth, Harold, Flexner, Stuart Berg. (eds.) **A Dictionary of American Slang.** N.Y. Crowell, 1960.

Proverbs and Sayings

(Dichos)

Innumerable sayings are Spanish and many of Mexican origin. The sayings have a feeling of the problems of life, and nature, confused, uncritical proverb. There is truth and principles concretely and wisdom of life which we can learn from popular proverbs is one of thousandfold observation, reflection and irony:

Cada loco con su tema.
A boca cerada no entra mosca.
Cada oveja con su pareja.
Cuando ven el palo caido todos quieren hacer lena.
Da y ten y haras bien.
Dime con quien andas y te dire quien eres.
El pan ajeno hace al hijo bueno.
Entre la espada y la pared.
Ir por lana y volver trasquilado.
Juntos pero no revueltos.
Le dan en el codo y aprieta la mano.
Lo que se hereda no se hurta.
Los muertos al pozo y los vivos al negocio.

Mas vale andar solo que mal acompanado.
Mas vale tarde que nunca.
Mas vale tuerto que ciego.
Mas vale mano que fuerza.
No hay mal que por bien no venga, ni enferme-
    dad que dure cien anos.
Panza llena corazon contento.
Pobre del pobre que al cielo no va, lo friegan
    aqui y lo friegan alla.
Santo que no es visto no es adorado.
Habla hasta por los codos.
No hay borracho que coma lumbre.
 Se me hace chico el mar para un buche de agua!
Tener suerte de gato boca arriba.
Perro que ladra no muerde.
Por uno que madruga, hay otro que no se acues-
    tra.
A la vista del amo, engorda el caballa.
Favores Referidos no son agradesidos.
Acada gallo se le llega su dia.
Si te cai el saco, pontelo.
El que no se mueve se lo lleva la corriente.
Las piedras rodando se encuentran.
Ojos que no ven corazon que no siente.
Hasta lo que no comes te hace dano.
Detras de la cruz esta el diablo.
La zorra nunca se ve la cola.
Entre el dicho y el hecho esta el trecho.
No fijetion no notation.
Afuerza ni los zapatos.
Suerte te de Dios que dinero para quieres.
La vista es muy natural.
No es lo mismo ver que agarar.
Amor de lejos, amor de pendejos.
Tengo doce hijos, ay! y todos vivos; entre vivos y
    tontos todos comen.
Pagan justos por pecadores.
Si duermes con los perros te levantas con pulgas.
De lo que te sobra repartes.

Chiquito pero picoso.

Lismonero con garrote.

Ensieren sus gallinas que mi gallo anda suelto.

Cada cabeza es un mundo.

Naiden sabe lo que esta en la hoilla, nomas la que lo esta meniando.

Que me haga pendejo es una cosa y que hagan es otra cosa.

El que abarca mucho poco aprieta.

Mi casa es su casa.

Donde come uno, comen dos.

Vale mas ser pobre y ser feliz y no ser rico y ser infeliz.

Vale mas que haiga un loco y no dos.

Vale mas andar un camino por conocido y no por conocer.

El vivo vive del pendejo.

No quiero que me tegan miedo, nomas quiero que me respeten.

Arancar la mala yerba, no es crimen.

Nada mas se muere una vez en una vida.

Con la vara que mides seras midido.

La mentira dura mientras que la verdad llega.

El que a dos amos sirve con alguno queda mal.

El amor es ciego.

En todo estas menos en misa.

Riddles

We shall present only a sufficient number of say-ings in riddle-like form to give an idea of what they are like. The following riddles have been utilized by Chicanos for several generations, both in Mexico and the United States.

De San Juan quiero la palma,
De San Francisco el cordon,
De Santa Rita la espina,
De mi amante el corazon.

Hasta la lena del monte,
Tiene su separacion,
Una sirve para santos,
Y otro para hacer carbon.

El demonio son los hombres,
Dicen todas las mujeres,
Y luego estan deseando,
Que el demonio se las lleve.

Baila pero no en la harina.
Answer: Bailarina (Dancer)

Blanca como la nieve,
Prieta como el carbon,

Anda y no tiene pies,
Habla y no tiene boca.
    Answer: Una Carta (Letter)

Blanco fue mi nacimiento,
Me pintaron de colores,
He causado muchas muertes,
Y he empobrecido senores.
    Answer: Barajas (playing cards)

Ya ves cuan claro es,
Adiviname lo que es.
    Answer: Llaves (Keys)

un vieja larga y seca que le escure la manteca
    Answer: Vela (Candle)

Que tan largo es un zapato?
    Answer: Un pie largo (1 foot long)

Que puedes hacer que no miras?
    Answer: Ruido (Noise)

Que le dijo el huante a la mano?
    Answer: Te tengo cubrido (I've got you
    covered)

Tu eres mi hermano, pero yo no soy tu hermano.
Quien soy yo?
    Answer: Tu hermana (Your sister)

Que clace de vibora es como un centavo?
    Answer: La cabeza de cobre (Copper-head)

Que fruta esta retratada en un nicle?
    Answer: Datil (Date)

Lana sube y lana baja?
    Answer: Nabaja (Knife)

Chicano Folk Medicine

(Plantas Medicinales)

The utilization of herbs in our continent were recorded by our Indian ancestors since Pre-Columbian time. The practice of the cures today are indeed a fusion of the Indian-Hispanic belief, since practically all medicine men (e.g., Witch doctors, Curanderos, etc.) have utilized the art of magic, herbs, minerals, and other traditional items. The Curers are highly regarded because of their vast knowledge of herbal lore.

Chicano Folk disease is not always distinguished on the basis of symptoms. Most diagnoses rest on the nature of inter-personal conflicts experienced by the Chicano itself. The diagnosis and treatment fulfills valid function in easing the social cultural problems involved in an illness. There is a concept of the cause of sickness which is, that everything on this earth has the power to cause its own kind of ailments. Thus, utilizing herbs as a means to cure their sickness. There are four specific common sicknesses among Chicanos (e.g., Mexican Americans):

Mal de ojo Evil eye
Empacho A form of indigestion

Susto	Fright; scared
Molera caida	Fallen fontanel

The following are a few of today's Chicano Home Remedies:

Remedy (Herbs)	Problem
Manzania	Mild fever
Yerba del venado	Substitute for milk nourishment
Estafiate	Stomach ache
Cascara Sagrada	Mild indigestion
Soft regular soap	Fallen fontanel
La golondrina	Lacerated penis
Masto	Stomach problems, bad indigestion
Avecol	Kidney problems; urinary problems
Tekin	Bad breath; lack of appetite
Japones	High blood pressure, circulation of the blood
Claudorita	Diabetes (sugar in the blood)
Brasil	Female menstrual problems
Jabon virtual	Scalp problems, rash and loss of hair
Mayacin	Weight problem
Jovel	Asthma and lung problems
Anis yerba anis	Fright, scared
Bergel	Sore muscles
Maravilla de chiapas	Stomach problems provoked by a nervous system
Azteca	Anemic
Talin	Nervous system attack

Lagrimas de San Pedro	To control the frequent urine of a diabetic
Polvo Argentino	Valve movement
Betel (Tizana)	Epileptic attacks, rapid pulse, anxiety
Raiz de Oro	Blisters (mouth), molar pains
Lucum	Intestinal parasites
12 Flores	Chronic, nervous attacks
Zimin	Low blood pressure
San Ignacio	An adult laxative

Chicano Folk Songs

La ``musica is the manifestation of the soul of any people. It is also a sincere feeling and humble inception. Chicano music (e.g., Corridos, Polkas, love themes, etc.) is simple in its construction and lasting in theme. Numerous Mexican songs of the past (e.g., Mexican Revolution, 1910) have created a moral and spiritual impact on the contemporary Chicano of today. A notable characteristic in the Chicano folk songs is the fact that they have not remained static in conformity with the social economical changes that occurred in the course of the past. The Southwest is regional, it adapts songs of neighboring countries to its tempo and rhythm. Its adaptation and popularity within our continent (e.g., America's) can be traced to the ability of rebirth on foreign soil.

Culturally and linguistically, Mexico and the Southwest of the United States have seldom been separated by their international borders. The Folk songs of Mexico are unmindful of the international boundaries, since in the songs of those regional areas, by the obliviously, ``Yo soy Mejicano de aqui de este lado,'' ``Que legos estoy del suelo donde he nacido,'' and,

"Si muero legos de aqui," stands as facts that culturally and linguistically, Chicanos on both sides of the border have remained identical.

We will attempt to list those songs considered relevant and popular in the United States by some Chicanos. The following list include songs such as "Adelita," "La Cucaracha," and "La Valentina." It should be noted that Revolutionary songs which are sung by Chicanos have endless number of verses since each Folklorist makes up new ones (e.g., words), and again, there are certain regional verses to each song. We decided to include those specific endless verses of our compadre Professor Jose Villarino of San Diego State University (e.g., for originality of each song, please see any Mexican "cancionero"). Each country has its Robinhood and the Chicanos have their Corridos (e.g., ballads of famous people). Corridos are the most popular type of music in the Southwest and again, it should be understood that each regional area has its own style. There are, as we mentioned before, hundreds of Chicano songs that have been omitted because of the element of time in completing our concise Chicano Dictionary.

*Those endless number of verses in our text were recreated by Mr. Jose Villarino of San Diego State University. The original composer of those songs were omitted because of two factors (1) Public domain; (2) Endless verses style. For the original form, see Mexican song books.

Adelita
(Endless Verse of Josse Villarino)

En lo alto de una abrupta serrania
    donde estaba y acampado un regimiento,
una joven que valiente los seguia
porque estaba enamorado de un sargento.

Popular entre la tropa era Adelita,
    la mujer por el sargento idolatrada

porque a mas de ser valientr era bonita
y hasta el mismo coronel la respetaba,
y se cuenta que decia el cuanto la queria:

Si Adelita se fuera con otro
　　le seguiria las huellas sin cesar,
si por mar en un buque de guerra,
si por tierra en un tren militar.

Si Adelita ha de ser mi esposa,
si Adelita ha de ser mi mujer,
Adelita, Adelita del alma,
Adelita de mi corazon.

Si Adelita quisiera ser mi esposa,
　　si Adelita fuera mi mujer,
le compraria un vestido de seda,
para llevarla a bailar al cuartel.

Adelita, por Dios te lo ruego,
　　calma el fuego de esta mi pasion,
porque te amo y te quiero rendido
y por ti sufre mi fiel corazon.

Si Adelita se fuera con otro
　　le seguiria las huellas sin cesar,
si por mar en un buque de guerra,
si por tierra en un tren militar.

Toca el clarin de campana a la guerra,
　　sale el valiente guerrero a pelear,
correran los arroyos de sangre,
　Que gobierne un tirano jamas!

Y si acaso yo muero en campana
　　y mi cuerpo en la sierra va a quedar,
Adelita, por Dios to lo ruego,
con tus ojos me vas a llorar.

La Cucaracha

(Endless Verse of Jose Villarino)

Coro:
La cucaracha, La cucaracha,
     Ya no puede caminar;
porque le falta, porque no tiene
marihuana que fumar.

Un panadero fue a misa,
     no encontrando que rezar,
entonces le podio a la virgen pura,
marihuana pa fumar.

O, hermosa San Jose!
     O, bonita Santa Ana!
dale permiso a tu hijo,
que fume su marihuana.

De por alla abajo vengo
     cansada de caminar;
me monte en un burro muerto
y no me pudo tirar.

Tengo un amigo listo
     que esta en el ayuntamento
y que tiene la exclusiva
para un nuevo pavimento.

Una mujer fue la causa
de mi perdicion primera,
y tambien de la segunda,
y tambien de la tercera.

De las barbas de Carranza
     voy hacer una toquilla,
Pa ponerla en el sombrero
del valiente Pancho Villa.

Ya murio la cucaracha,
    ya la llevan a enterrar,
entre cuatro zapilotes
y un raton de sacristan.

Una cosa me da risa:
    Pancho Villa sin camisa;
Ya se van los Carranzistas,
porque vienen los Villistas.

Necesito un automovil
    para hacer la caminato
al lagar donde, mando
a la convencion Zapata.

Para sarapes, Saltillo,
Chihuahua para soldados,
para mujers, Jalisco;
para amor, toditos lados.

La Valentina
(Endless Verse of Jose Villarino)

Una pasion me domina,
    es la que me ha hecho venir,
Valentina, Valentina,
yo te quisiera decir:

Dicen que por tus amores
    un mal me van a seguir,
no le hace que sean el diablo,
yo tambien me si morir.

Si porque bebo tequila,
    manana bebo jerez,
si porque me ves borracho,
manana ya no me ves:

Valentina, Valentina,
     rendido estoy a tus pies,
si me han de matar manana,
que me maten de una vez.

Gabino Barrera
(Endless Verse of Jose Villarino)

Gabino Barrera con mas de
     Mil hombres, se por las sierras.

Su causa era buena, pelear
     Por los pobres, . . . y repartirles
la tierra.

Usaba el bigote, grandote apufado
     Su pano rojo enredado
Vestido de manta, Hablo con Madero,
Traia riscando el sombrero.

Sus pies campesinos, usaban guaraches
y aveces a raiz andaba.
Pero aunque pisaba sobre los
Huisaches sus plantos no se espinaban.

Con una botella de cana en la mano,
     Gritaba Viva Zapata porque era ranchero
El indio suriano era hijo de buena mata.

Era muy bien dado, muy ancho de espalda,
     Surostro mal encachado sus cejas cerradas
Parecian las alas de guitre de las montanas.

Gabino Barrera igual que Zapata queria
     Repartir las tierras por eso peleaba y
Entraba en batallas sonando sus carrieras.

Recuerdo la noche que los asesinaron a un
Lado de Hatehuala 18 descargos de mauser
      donaron
Sin darle tiempo de nada.

Gabino Barrera con todo y caballa cayo
    Con la balaser, la cara de un Hombre revolusion-
     ario,
quedo besando la tierra.

La Llorona
(Endless Verse by Jose Villarino)

La pena y la que no es pena, ay llorona,
    Todo es pena para mi;
Ayer lloraba por verte, ay llorona,
Y hoy lloro porque te vi.

Salias del templo un dia, ay llorona,
    Cuando al pasar yo te vi.
Hermosa huipil con blondas llevabas
Que la Virgen te crei.

Me subi al pino mas alto, ay llorona,
    A ver si te divisaba.
Como el pino era tierno, ay llorona,
Al verme llorar, lloraba.

Cada vez que entra la noche, ay llorona,
    Me pongo a pensar y digo:
De que me sirve la cama, ay llorona,
Si tu no duermes conmigo.

Ay di me, llorona, llorona,
    Llorona de azul turqui,
Ayer lloraba por verte, ay llorona,
Y hoy lloro porque te vi.

De la mar vino una carta, ay llorona,
    Que me mando la sirena,

Y en la carta me decia, ay llorona,
Quien tiene amor tiene pena.

La pena y la que no es pena, ay llorona,
Todo es pena para mi.
Ayer lloraba por verte, ay llorona,
Y hoy lloro porque te vi.

Ay de mi, llorona, llorona,
    Llorona de azul celeste,
Aunque la vida me cueste, ay llorona,
No dejare de querete.

La Llorona (Huapangos)
(Endless Verse of Jose Villarino)

Se repite: Todos me dicen el negro llorona
            Negro pero carinoso

Se repite: Yo soy como el chile verde llorona
            Picante pero sabroso

Se repite: Ay de mi llorona llorona
            Llorona de azul celeste

Se repite: Aunque la vida me cueste llorona
            No dejare de quererte

Se repite: Dicen que no tengo duelo llorona
            Porque no me ven llorar

Se repite: Hay muertos que no hacen ruido llorona
            Y es mas grande su penar

Se repite: Ay de mi llorona llorona
            Llorona de ayer y hoy

Se repite: Ayer maravilla fui llorona
            Y ahora ni sombra soy.

English-Chicano-Hispano
Index

A

Absent-minded - **ATRAN-TADO** 23
Activities - **HUATO** 48
Adventurer - **ANDARIEGO** .21
Afraid - **CHIVA** 34
Afro, black - **MAYATE,
TINTO** 57
Air - **AIGRE** 20
Airplane - **AUROPLANO** 23
Alcoholic beverage -
PISTO 64
Alert - **AL ALBA** 20
Alienate - **CORTARSE** 37
Alone - **ANDAR SOLARES** . .21
Anger - **CACHAS, CAL-
DIADO** 28, 29
Angie - **KELA** 51
Anglocized - **AGRINGADO** . 19
Anglo-Saxon - **AMERI-
CANO, GRINGO** 21
Appeals - **ME CUADRA** 57
Appetizer - **BOTANA** 27
Appreciate, like - **QUA-
DRAR** 66

Argument, discussion - **RE-
PELIDO** 68
Arizona - **ARAIZA** 22
Army Sergeant - **SARDO**. 70
Arnold - **NONO** 59
Arrest - **TORCER** 76
Astray - **NO TE RESVALES** . . .60
Arthur Pearl - **ARTURO
PERLA** 22
Auto - **RAMFLA** 67
Automobile - **CARRUCHA** . .31

B

Baby-sitter - **PILMAMA** 64
Back-up - **ESQUINIAR** 43
Bad luck - **SALADO** 70
Balloon - **BOMBA** 26
Bank - **MACIZO** 55
Base - **BEIS** 25
Baseball bat - **BATE** 24
Bowl - **SOFOQUE** 71
Bowl-out - **SOPLON** 71
Beans - **COCOLES** 35
Beat it! - **PINTATE** 64

Bee - **AVISPA** 23
Beer - **BIRONGA, BIRRIA,**
   BUFA 25. 27
Belt - **FAJA** 44
Bend - **PANDIARSE** 61
Bewitched - **EMBRUJADO** . . 41
Bill - **BIL** 25
Billfold - **BILLETERA** 25
Blackballed - **MARCA** 56
Black-listed - **CHOTIADO** . . . 34
Black sheep - **MANCHA**
   NEGRA 56
Blow - **GUAMASO** 47
Blowout - **BLOAUTE** 25
Bluff - **BLOFE** 25
Bootlegger - **BUTLEGER** 28
Border Patrol - **LA COREA** . . 52
Bother - **MOLAR** 58
Boy - **GUERCO** 48
Boy-friend - **CHAVO** 32
Brakes - **BRECAS** 27
Breast - **CHICHI** 33
Brother - **BRODA** 27
Brown noser - **BARBIAR** 24
Brushland - **MOGOTE** 58
Bullock - **BUEY** 27
Bumper-jack - **LLAQUE** 54
Bundle - **LIACHO** 54
Burp - **ORUTAR** 60
Bus - **BOS** 27
Butt - **BACHA** 24

C

Cake - **QUEIQUE** 66
California - **CALIFAS** 29
Calm down - **CALMALA** . . . 29
Camp - **CAMPIAR** 30
Cap - **CACHUCHA** 28
Captain - **CAPIRUCHO** 30
Car - **ROL** 68
Careful, watch out - **AGUAS** 19
Careless - **ATARANTADO** . . . 23
Cash - **LANA** 52
Catch - **QUECHAR** 66

Cement block - **BLOQUE** . . . 25
Cheat - **CHAPUCERO** 32
Chicano idiom - **TOTACHA** . 76
Chicken - **GALLINA** 46
Child - **CHAVALON** 32
Childbirth - **ALIVIARSE** 20
Christmas - **CRISMAS** 37
City lot - **LOTE** 55
Clan - **INDIADA** 49
Clothes diaper - **PANALES** . . 61
Clothes pins - **PALITOS** 61
Clothing - **GARRA** 46
Clown, impersonator -
   PANTOCHA 61
Clumsy - **CABALLO** 28
Coins - **FERIA** 44
Common weed - **QUELITE** . 66
Commotion - **LABERINTO** . 51
Consent, encourage -
   PAPACHAR 61
Contented - **YENO** 79
Convict - **PINTO** 64
Copy - **COPIAR** 36
Coquette - **PAJUELA** 61
Cotton gin - **YIN** 79
Crazy - **LUQUIS** 55
Creek - **CHARCO** 32
Crooked - **LANGARA** 53
Crowd - **BOLA** 26
Cry baby - **CHILLON** 33
Cure, fix - **CURA** 37
Curse - **RAYAR** 67

D

Dancing . **CHANCLIANDO** . 31
Date - **DATILE** 38
Day dreaming - **NUBES** 60
Dead - **ATIRANTADO** 23
Defraud - **CHAPUSIAR** 32
Depot - **DIPO** 40
Detention center - **TARIS** . . . 73
Diapers - **MANTILLAS** 56
Dice - **HUEZOS** 49
Dike, ditch - **BORDO** 26

Dime - **DAIME** 38
Dirty, waste - **MIERDA** 58
Disagreement - **VERI-
GUATE** 79
Disgrace, ridicule - **RELAJER** 68
Dismiss - **DAR SU CHEQUE** . . 38
Doll - **MONA** 58
Dory - **DORIA** 40
Dressing, mode - **TRAZAS** . . 76
Drink - **PAJUELAZO** 61
Drinking spree - **PAR-
RANDA** 62
Drive - **ARRIAR** 22
Drunkard - **BORRACHALES** . 26
Dumb, silly - **TARUGO** 73
Dump truck - **DOMPE** 40

E

Easy, good - **SUAVE** 71
Easy make - **PICHON** 63
Eat - **REFINAR** 68
Edinburg - **LIMBURGO** 54
Egg - **BLANQUILLO** 25
Elope - **SE HULLO** 70
Encouragement - **AHUI-
CHOTIAR** 20
Enough - **YA ESTUFAS** 79
Enter - **PASALE** 62
Eraser - **BORRADOR** 26
Escape - **PELARSE** 63
Eugene - **KENO** 51
Evil eye - **MAL DE OJO** 56
Examiner, tester - **TESTA-
DOR** 74
Exchange - **CAMBALACHE** . 29
Extremely good - **DE
AQUELLA** 39
Eye - **VIRULO** 79

F

Faker - **PAPELERO** 62
Fan, windmaker - **ABAN-
ICO** 19

Father - **JEFE** 50
Feet, foot - **PESUNA** 63
Female dog - **BUSGA** 28
Feminish male - **MARICON** . 57
Festivity - **FANDANGO,
PACHANGA** 44, 60
Fire engine - **APAGADORA** . 21
Flabby - **MASA** 57
Flirt - **CARITA, VACILAR** . . 3, 78
Flunk - **FLONQUIAR** 45
Flush - **FLOCHIAR** 45
Fool - **FULIAR** 46
Free-loaders - **ALGODON-
ERAS** 20
French bread - **BIROTE** 25
Friend - **COMPA** 36
Frustrated, disgusted -
AGUITADO 19
Furniture, baggage - **TILI-
CHES** 74

G

Gang - **GANGA** 46
Garage - **GARAJE** 46
Gasoline - **GASOFA** 47
Girl - **HUIZA** 49
Go ahead - **DAR LUZ,
PICALE** 38, 63
Golf - **GOLFO** 47
Good - **BRUTAL** 27
Gosh! - **ILO!** 49
Gossip - **CHISME** 34
Grade - **GRADO** 47
Groceries - **GROCERIAS** 47
Group - **BONCHE** 26
Guitar - **LIRA** 54
Gum - **GOMA** 47
Guy - **BATO** 24
Gypsy - **HUNGARO** 49

H

Hail - **GRANIZO** 47
Hair - **GRENA** 47

Hairy - **PACHON** 60
Half dollar - **TOSTON** 76
Hamburger - **HAMBOR-
GESA** 48
Hand - **BAISA** 24
Handshake - **CHOCALA** 34
Harrassment - **DANDO
CARRILLA** 38
Harvest - **PIZCA** 65
Hat - **SOMBRERO, TAR-
LANGO** 73
Hateful - **CHOCANTE,
SANGRON** 34, 70
Healthy - **BIEN DADO** 25
Heavy eater - **TRAGON** 76
Hello - **ALO** 20
Henrietta - **KETA** 51
Herbalist - **YERBERO** 79
Herion - **EL AZUFRE** 40
Hey! - **EIT!** 40
Hey you! - **ESE!** 42
High, drugs - **ALIVIANADO** . 20
Hint - **PUNTADA** 66
Hippy - **MECHUDO** 57
Hitchhiking - **CON EL
GORDO** 36
Hobo - **BALDE** 24
Hog pen - **CHIQUERO** 33
Hog wash - **PURO PEDO** . . . 66
Home, pad - **CHANTE** 32
Hoodlum - **RAQUETERO** 67
Hook - **GANCHAR** 46
Hope so - **OJALA** 60
Hop scotch - **BEBE LECHE** . . . 25
House - **CANTON** 30
Hurry - **ATIZAR** 23
Hustle - **TALONIAR** 72

I

Ice plant - **HIELERIA** 48
Idiom - **CALO** 29
Ignorant - **TAPADO** 73
Ignore - **AVENTAR A LOCO** . 23
Imbecile - **BABOSO** 24
Infant - **ESQUINCLE** 43

Inhale - **TOQUE** 76
In love - **ENCANICADO** 42
Instigator - **BORLOTERO** . . . 26
Insult - **ATACON** 23
Iodine - **SANGRE DE
CHANGO** 70
It's cool - **ESTA PADRE** 43

J

Jail - **EL BOTE, TABIQUE** . 40, 72
Jake, Joaquin - **KINO** 51
Jealous - **ARISCO** 22
Jeep - **YIPE** 79
Job - **CHAMBA** 31
Joke - **SONSIAR** 71
Junior - **NUNE** 60

K

Kick - **BOTAR** 27
Kindergarten - **QUINDER** . . . 67
Kinfolks, relatives - **PARI-
ENTES** 62
Kissed - **BESOTIO** 25
Kite - **PAPALOTE** 61
Knife - **FILA** 45
Knockout - **NOCAUT** 59

L

Law - **JURADO** 51
Laziness - **FLOJERA** 45
Lazy - **HUEVON, FLO-
JERA** 49, 45
Leak - **LIQUIAR** 54
Left-handed - **ZURDAZO** . . . 80
Lie, myth - **LINEA** 54
Life style - **HONDA** 48
Lift, ride - **ABENTON** 19
Light skin - **APERLADO** 22
Load, batch - **CARGA** 30
Loaf - **FLOJIAR** 45
Los Angeles - **LOS** 55

Loudmouth - **BOCON** 25
Lousy - **TIRADO** 75
Lubbock - **LOBICA** 54
Lucky - **SUERTUDO** 72
Lunch - **LONCHE** 55
Lunch box - **LONCHERA** 55
Lure. set up - **CANDILAR** . . .30

M

Magazine - **MAGACIN** 56
Maid. housekeeper - **GATA** 47
Malnutrition - **TRASASAM-
BRIDO** 76
Manhandle - **MANOSIAR** . . .56
Marijuana - **GRIFA** 47
Married - **AMARADO** 20
Matches - **MECHAS** 57
Match. game - **MECHAR** . . 57
Me - **YOGAS** 80
Meddling - **METICHE** 57
Mess up - **REGARLA** 68
Mexican American - **CHI-
CANO** 33
Mexican border - **AL OTRO
LADO** 20
Mexico, Mexican - **MEJICLE** .57
Midget - **ENANO** 41
Midwife - **COMADRONA,
PARTERA** 36, 62
Miss - **MISTIAR** 58
Mistake, foul - **PENDEJIAR** . .63
Money - **BICA, JANDO** . . 25, 50
Moody - **CACHUDO** 28
Mother - **JEFA** 50
Mouth - **HOCICO** 48
Movies, theatre - **EL
MONO** 41
Mud - **ZOQUETE** 80
Muddy - **ZOQUETOSO** 80
Muffler - **MOFLE** 58
Mulato - **QUARTERON** 66

N

Nahuatl Nation - **AZTLAN** . . 24
Narrow-minded - **BIEN
CERRADO** 25
Negro, black - **TIRACHO,
MAYATE** 75
Neighborhood - **BARRIO,
VECINDAD** 24
Nelly - **AIDANELA** 20
Noise - **TRACALADA** 76
Now - **ORITA!** 60
Number one - **MERO BEBE** .57

O

Observe - **LICORIAR** 54
Odd Ball - **CALABURNIA** . . .29
O.K., Alright - **A TODO DAR** 23
Old man - **TAYUDO** 73
Overshoes - **SOBRES** 71

P

Panties - **PANTALETAS** 61
Pants - **ESTRAMOS, TRA-
MADOS** 43, 76
Paper - **PAPIRO** 62
Park - **PARQUE** 62
Party, celebration - **MITOTE** 58
Pass out - **NOQUIADO** 59
Peer group - **PALOMIA** 61
Penny - **CLEMO** 35
Pepper - **CHILIQUIPIN** 33
Persistent - **TERQUIAR** 74
Pick - **TALACHE** 72
Picture - **RETRA** 68
Pimp - **PADROTE** 61
Pinch - **PELISCAR** 63
Pipe - **PAIPA, PIPA** 61, 64
Pitch - **PICHAR** 63
Point - **PUNTA** 66
Policeman. cop - **AZUL,
CHOTA** 24

Pot - **MOTA** 58
Psychofanting - **DAR**
  MADERA 38
Punches - **GOLPES** 47
Puppy - **POPE** 65
Purse - **BOLSA** 26
Push - **PUCHAR** 66

Q

Queer - **FRESCO** 45
Quickly - **ZUMBARSE** 80

R

Radio - **PERICA** 63
Raggedy looking -
  GARRERO 46
Rap - **COTORRIAR** 37
Record - **PLATO** 65
Refrigerator - **HIELERIA** 48
Rim - **RIN** 68
Ring - **HUEZO** 49
Rubber shoes - **HULES** 49
Ruin - **AMOLADO** 21
Ruler - **RULA** 69

S

Scar - **MALANCON** 56
Scram - **AVOLAR** 23
Seal, tape - **TEIPIAR** 73
Sell out - **BENDIDO** 25
Settle down - **ANCLIAR** 21
Sewer - **DRENAJE** 40
Sexy female - **CAJETUDA** . . . 28
Shack - **TICURUCHO** 74
Sharp, alert - **ABUSADO** 19
Sheriff - **CHERIFE** 32
Shirt - **LIZA** 54
Shoes - **CALCOS** 29
Sick - **MALANCON** 56
Silly, bored - **SURA** 72
Skull, head - **QUENCA** 66

Slap - **CACHETADA** 28
Slice, cut - **TASAJIAR** 73
Slip down - **SUELAZO** 71
Sloppy looking - **FACHOSO** 44
Slow-poke - **PACHORO** . . . 60
Smell - **AOLER** 21
Smoke - **CHUPAR** 35
Smoking - **TABAQUIADO** . . . 72
Snack, food - **PIPIRIN** 64
Sneaky - **LARGO** 53
Snickers - **CHUPA, CHAR-**
  COS 35
Soul brothers - **CARNAL** . . . 30
Sour - **CURSI** 38
Spank - **NALGIAR** 59
Spark plug - **CHISPA** 34
Spell - **ESPELIAR** 42
Spoiled infant - **CHIPON** . . . 33
Square - **VENADO** 78
Stamp - **ESTAMPA** 43
Stand-out - **RIFARSE** 68
Stare - **FISGIAR** 45
Statement - **FREGADERA** . . 45
Steal - **CLAVAR** 35
Stingy - **PICHICATE** 63
Stocky - **CHAPARRA** 32
Stomach - **BARRIGA** 24
Stoned - **MOTIADO** 59
Stood-up - **PLANTADO** 65
Store - **TENDAJO** 74
Store owner - **TENDAJERO** . 73
Stretch - **TENDIDO** 74
Strike - **SONAR** 71
Strong, heavy - **LECHUDO** . . 53
Strong character - **TANATES** 73
Stubborn, alert - **ABUSADO** . 19
Stupid - **ATASCADO, PEN-**
  DEJO 23, 63
Sturdy, straight - **TANDO** . . . 73
Suit - **TACUCHO** 72
Sweetheart, wife - **MI**
  PRIETA 58
Swing - **COLUMPIO** 36
Switch - **SWEE-CHI** 72
Switch Blade - **FILERA** 45

T

Talkative - **COTORRO** 37
Tall - **CEROTE** 31
Tame - **AMANSAR** 20
Take off - **BORRATE**.......26
Tattle tale - **CHISMOLERO** .34
Teach - **TICHAR** 74
Teaser-loose - **VALAS** 78
Temper, tantrum - **BERRIN-
  CHUDO(A)** 25
Tetanus, lockjaw - **MAL DE
  ARCO** 56
Texas Ranger - **RINCHE** 68
Theatre - **TIATRO, MONO** ..74
Thrill - **PATADA**............62
Thunder storm - **TRUENOS**..77
Tired person - **BOMBO** 26
To bluff - **BLOFIAR** 25
To fire - **DAR AIRE**.........38
To leave - **DESCONTARSE** ..39
Tom boy - **CHANGA,
  PINGA**...............31, 64
To spot - **ESPATIAR**........42
Tough, rough - **TOFUDO** ...75
Town, city - **TANGO** 73
Train - **EL RIELE**............41
Trap, trick - **GAITA**.........46
Trash, scum - **RASPA** 67
Trend, pattern - **HONDA** ...48
Tricky - **CARANCHO** 30
Trod - **AL TROTE** 20
Trouble - **BUSCAR PEDO**...27
Truck - **TROCA** 77
Twin - **CUATE, CUATA** 37
Type - **TAIPIAR**............72

U

Uncle Tom - **TIO TACO, TIO
  TOMAS**.................75
Unhumane - **BESTIA**........25

Unintelligent - **BURRO,
  BURRON, TOPO** 27, 75
Unworthy - **VALER
  SOQUETE** 78
U.S. Mexican American ·
  PONCHO...............65

V

Ventura - **VENTO** 79
Virile male - **MACHO**.......55

W

Wait - **APLOMO** 22
Walk - **APATIN** 21
Water boy - **AGUADOR** 19
Water pump - **POMPA** 65
Water Tower - **TINACO** 74
Wealthy - **LANUDO** 53
Well-versed - **AVENTADO** ..23
Wetback - **MOJADO** 58
Whole truth - **PURITITO**.....66
Wish - **ANIMAS**............21
Wreck - **CHOQUE** 34

X

Y

Yard - **YARDA** 79
Yell, cry out - **AGRITO** 14
Yes - **CIROL** 35
Junk - **YONQUE, YONKE**...80
Youngster - **TRIPON**........77

Z

Zoot-suiter - **PACHUCO** 60